JOHN MEYENDORFF was born in Neuilly-sur-Seine, France, in 1926 and educated at the University of Paris (Sorbonne). He graduated from the Orthodox Theological Institute, Paris, in 1950 and received a *Doctorat ès Lettres* from the University of Paris (Sorbonne) in 1958.

Ordained in 1959, Father Meyendorff served successively as Lecturer and Assistant Professor of Church History at the Orthodox Theological Institute, Paris. Currently he is Professor of Church History and Patristics, St. Vladimir's Orthodox Theological Seminary, Crestwood, New York.

A member of the Faith and Order Commission of the World Council of Churches, Father Meyendorff is also Visiting Professor, Department of History, Columbia University, Visiting Lecturer, Union Theological Seminary, and Lecturer, Harvard University, Dumbarton Oaks.

Orthodoxy and Catholicity

John Meyendorff

ORTHODOXY and CATHOLICITY

SHEED & WARD NEW YORK

This book appeared originally in French under the title,
Orthodoxie et Catholicité
© 1965, Editions du Seuil, Paris, France

Library of Congress Catalog Card Number 66-22017

Manufactured in the United States of America

Foreword

Under the general title, *Orthodoxy and Catholicity*, we offer the text of several studies which we have had published in various periodicals between 1954 and 1965. As these studies appear in the present volume, they have been brought up to the moment both in content and bibliography.

The unity among the chapters here is not to be found in style or method. Some of the chapters represent historical research and include discussions of technicalities; others treat of general problems with which the average reader is familiar. Rather, the unity of this collection lies elsewhere: all articles are devoted to one or another problem of Christian unity. Throughout the pages which follow, the effort has been, first, to bring to the fore and to examine those issues which emerge from a confrontation between the Orthodox Church, on the one hand,

and Roman Catholicism and Protestantism on the other: secondly, to examine critically the contemporary Orthodox witness in the West.

The author's conviction is that the notion of the Church's "catholicity," which all Christians nominally confess, is a central one for the understanding both of what authentic ecumenism should be and of the mission of the Orthodox Church in the world today. To "ecumenists" reminder is given that Christian unity cannot be the result of human efforts only; it can neither be "organized" nor "negotiated." Its very reality resides in a direct experience of a living and incarnate God, for, as Ignatius of Antioch wrote, "Where Christ Jesus is, there is the Catholic Church."

Unity, therefore, presupposes the presence of Christ Himself; it is unity with Him, first, and then also unity with others. His presence implies the acceptance of His truth in its fullness.

Moreover, the "catholicity" of the Church judges also those who claim that they already possess the full truth. For what is the truth—especially Christ's truth—if it is not viable, valuable and acceptable to all, if those who confess it with their lips disfigure it in their day-by-day behavior?

Ultimately implied in the note of Catholicity is the fact that the Church has no separate and autonomous existence outside of Christ and the Holy Spirit acting in the world and for the world. Accordingly, its catholicity is inseparable from its other notes of holiness, unity, apostolicity. A true Orthodox contribution to the contemporary ecumenical movement must aim at the recovery of this Christocentric and Spirit-centered view of the Church, without which ecumenism loses its very meaning.

CONTENTS

Orthodoxy
and
Catholicity

I

*Sacraments and Hierarchy**

The dialogue on ecclesiology, which opened after the publication of Oscar Cullmann's book on St. Peter,[1] flatly contradicted all those who still despaired of a better understanding between theologians in the Reformation tradition and those who belong to the Catholic tradition. The problem of the history of salvation, already raised by Cullman in earlier works, was considered during this dialogue from various points of view, and, in a more particular way, from that which is central to this debate: What is the relationship between the unique sacrifice of Christ and his presence in the Church? Most of the problems which nowadays separate Christians flow, in effect, from the answers given by one or others to that question, whether it be the role of Tradition, of apostolic succession, or of the Sacraments.

*Originally published in French in *Dieu Vivant,* 26, 1954, pp. 89–91.

In these pages we should like to investigate how these different questions are linked together. Western medieval theology often and improperly put them into separate compartments; in so doing, these theologians caused the reaction of the Reformers who, in some instances, were satisfied with suppressing those compartments which seemed to them to have no direct link with the New Testament message. In particular, this was especially the case with the Sacraments and Tradition.

By giving back to the Sacraments the place which they deserve in the New Testament,[2] Professor Cullmann resets the ecclesiological problem in its fullness, and not from one point of view only. In fact, we believe that the problems of Tradition and of the post-apostolic hierarchy are closely and inseparably linked with the sacramental nature of the Church on the level of history as well as of doctrine. On the organic and sacramental nature of the Church depend the living and uninterrupted presence of truth within it and the existence of necessary "order." This relationship between the sacramental nature of the Church and the hierarchical order is nowadays generally recognized even by those who reject both as genuine elements of the Christian message.[3] If, in his book on Tradition, Cullman refuses to link the doctrine of a teaching hierarchy with his doctrine of the Sacraments, the reason is that he sees apostolic succession as a kind of co-option of individuals into the college of the apostles, an impossibility according to New Testament understanding of apostleship.[4]

Roman Catholic exegesis considers Matthew 16:18 (the building of the Church on Peter) as the expression of an essential principle of this ecclesiastical order. Undoubtedly no serious exegesis (unless it denies its almost unquestionable authenticity) can refuse to give an exceptional importance to this verse in which Christ expressly speaks about the future of the community which he intends to start. However, the problem of exegesis raised by this passage cannot be reduced to the question of whether the Church's foundation is the *faith* of Peter (according to the ancient and unanimous patristic tradition followed by the Reformers) or Peter himself. Catholic critics of Cullmann have rightly pointed out the main problem: Can Peter have a successor? For, as far as Catholic—and Orthodox—tradition is concerned, one cannot speak about the Church without implying an uninterrupted continuity through history. Consequently, we must start by an investigation of the precise meaning which the Lord intended to give to the central reality about which Matthew's verse spoke: the Church. The meaning we ascribe to that word will determine our understanding of its foundation on Peter.

According to Catholic tradition, in contrast with that which issued from the Reformation, the Church is an organic and sacramental reality which actualizes throughout history the work acomplished by Christ once and for all at a particular moment in time. Christ is really present in the Christian community. His presence constitutes the Mystery of Christ and of the Church: it gives back to mankind its lost intimacy with the Father and it anticipates the second coming of the Son of Man. But when we apply to that organic and sacramental reality the Pauline theology of the Church as the Body of Christ, let us remember that the Church, as an organic reality, is, first of all, the local eucharistic gathering, the "Church of God which is in Corinth" (1 Corinthians 1:2; 2 Corinthians 1:1 ff.), in Rome or Antioch. When St. Paul speaks of "members" of that Church, he always and exclusively means persons, not communities, for communities are churches (Galatians 1:2) and the Body of Christ is actualized in them in its totality. There is no room in this article to investigate whether *ekklesia* in the New Testament means only the local Christian assembly;[5] however, to consider Christ's presence within a local community as only partial would be utterly alien to Pauline theology. However, one is led to such a view if he thinks of the Church primarily as a geographically universal organic entity of which local communities are only parts.[6] If such an entity is genuinely the Body of Christ, then the Churches of Corinth, Jerusalem, or Rome are portions of it, and it is natural for Rome to function as the head. Could that correspond to the view of St. Ignatius of Antioch for whom "where is Christ Jesus, there is the Catholic Church"[7]—in other words, the whole body of Christ, represented by the local eucharistic community, with the bishop as its head?

This remark brings to light the relationship between apostleship and the apostolic hierarchy which derived from it. Historically an unmistakable fact distinguishes apostles from bishops right from the beginning: apostles derived from Christ a universal mission to preach (Matthew 28:19),[8] while bishops, both during the apostles' life and after their death, had a pastoral field limited to one local community. It is a questionable argument, and too easy a way out, to ascribe the difference purely to convenience. The right approach sees there a necessity of ecclesiology: without denying the link of succession between the two ministries, it defines each according to its function.

As living and direct witnesses to Christ's resurrection, the Twelve dedicated themselves, first of all, to preaching the Gospel. Their ministry coincided with their function as witnesses to a historical fact of universal significance:

in that function no one could replace them. Their role was not to preside over local communities, but to announce the Gospel to the whole universe. They had the power to administer the sacraments, but they did not normally exercise it: St. Paul's ministry was reckoned identical with theirs, and he "was not sent to baptize" (1 Corinthians 1:17). Primarily, their mission was to establish churches organized after a pattern which appears to be uniform by the beginning of the second century and which is defined by the sacramental nature of Christ's presence in the Church.

The documents at our disposal do not give us any certainty about the existence of a "monarchical episcopate" in all the Churches from the first century;[9] some communities may have been presided over by a college of presbyters. On the other hand, we can assert that there never was a Christian Church where the Lord's Supper was not celebrated. Whether we examine the texts about the Jerusalem Mother Church or those describing the Pauline communities dispersed around the Mediterranean, we find everywhere the supreme role played by the local assembly of Christians gathered for the eucharistic supper. Of necessity, someone had to take the Lord's place in each assembly. We do not know whether in some Churches this place was not held by the presbyters in turn, but we do know that at the beginning of the second century Ignatius of Antioch speaks of the episcopate as a self-evident institution and that Irenaeus will soon after draw up episcopal lists for all the churches dispersed throughout the whole Roman world.

St. Ignatius' doctrine of the episcopate is well known: "he takes the place of God by presiding over the community"[10] while the presbyters around him represent the apostles. The Lord's Supper is thus fully reproduced in each Christian community. The bishop's authority is exercised within the assembly and according to his place in the assembly: his place is that of God, and no place is higher.

Consequently the Church soon gave the bishop the title of "high priest" (*archiereus*), reserved for Christ alone in the Epistle to the Hebrews, because the bishop is the image of Christ amidst an assembly of kings and sacrificers (I Peter 2:9; Revelation 1:6; 5:10; 20:6); he is, therefore, also mediator, spouse and father. This essentially sacramental and liturgical nature of the episcopal function is indirectly confirmed by the data Irenaeus gives on apostolic succession in the primitive Church. The bishop's "apostolicity," according to Irenaeus, is primarily understood as a criterion of true doctrine and is transmitted through the succession of bishops in one and the same local church, originally established by the apostles.[11] The "sure charism of truth,"[12] possessed by all bishops, is intrinsically linked with the community's mystery spreading through history the historical event of which the apostles were the witnesses: side by side with Christ's other ministries, the bishop exercises also that of teaching, of which apostolic succession is both a condition and a manifestation.[13] But that truth must necessarily be the *same* in all episcopal eucharistic communities, for everywhere the same Catholic Church must recognize itself in its absolute uniqueness. As early as the third century it appears clearly that no bishop can be consecrated unless other bishops meet in his church and take part in his installation.

An ecclesiology which is based on the presence of catholic plenitude in each church, and such was undoubtedly the early Christian ecclesiology, leads in no way to the fragmentation of the ecclesiastical organism. The unity of Christians in the universe does not exist because the various churches complement one another; it is realised, above all, in the identity of faith, manifested, in turn, in sacramental communion. The author believes it is impossible to find a criterion of unity other than that, not only during the pre-Constantinian period, but also during the great doctrinal controversies of the later times.

From another point of view, this ecclesiology seems to solve at least a number of difficulties experienced by Reformed Christians who, even when they accept the sacramental aspect of Christianity, are repelled by the doctrine of apostolic succession conceived solely as the perpetuation of the apostolic charisma personally transmitted from one individual to another. In fact, a sacramental ecclesiology presupposes succession from the very fact of the objective identity which must exist between the Christian assembly of the apostles' time and that in existence in the twentieth century: but such a succession cannot be thought of as above or outside the eucharistic community which constitutes the Church.

It has been pointed out above that neither the Twelve nor St. Paul normally exercised permanent functions in a given local community. Yet there seems to have been an exception of major importance: that of Peter in the primitive community of Jerusalem, according to the narrative of the first twelve chapters of Acts. It was most certainly Peter who presided over the common eucharistic assembly which gathered round the apostles the whole of the first Christian community.[14] He was the first, probably on the day of Pentecost, to take the Lord's place at the celebration of the Supper. He thus inaugurated a new period in the history of salvation, that of Christ's presence in the Mystery among his own, at the moment when they accomplish what he commanded them to do in remembrance of him and in expectation of his second coming.

Obviously, as Cullmann points out,[15] one cannot speak of an episcopate of Peter in Jerusalem without taking into account the exceptional role, not comparable with that of the later presbyterate, which the apostles played by Peter's side. This is especially true if one looks at the episcopate from the point of view of pastoral authority. But the unique liturgical function which Peter alone could hold when the *whole* Church was gathered (*homou pantes*)—if one does not go beyond the first twelve chapters of Acts—certainly gave him an absolutely exceptional position which is reflected in the pages of the New Testament. One could wonder whether the words of Jesus, recorded only in Matthew's Gospel, were not precisely preserved in Palestine, where Matthew's Gospel originated, for the reason that they dealt with the role of Peter in the original Judeo-Christian community of Jerusalem.[16] This would be the obvious meaning of Matthew 16:18 if it is recognized that the original meaning of the word is the local community which, in Matthew's Gospel, is primarily the Jerusalem community. The logion of Matthew 16:18, even if it does not directly mention a "succession" to Peter, must, however, apply to all those who held in the Church the same functions which Peter had in Jerusalem, in the several communities created by the apostles in the Roman world, after the model of the Upper Room.

However, as Cullmann points out, Peter certainly abandoned the direction of the Jerusalem community. For we see him go away to "another place" (Acts 12:17), and this passage acquires an even more direct meaning if one remembers the life-long nature which the presidential functions were to acquire from the beginning in the

Christian assembly. The fact of going away "to another place" unmistakably meant that another was to sit in the Lord's place within the assembly. We know the name of that other one: James, the brother of the Lord, the first successor of Peter at the head of the Jerusalem community. It does not appear, however, that Peter should have been reduced to a missionary state, in dependence to the Church he had presided over until then, as Cullmann suggests. From that moment, the Twelve became conscious of their universal mission as living witnesses to the Resurrection, and Peter could not give up his "first" place within their college. The passages which describe for us the relationship between Peter and James (Acts 12:17; 15:6 ff; Galatians 2:9–12) provide significant testimonies of the mutual interdependance of the apostolic ministry and the sacramental ministry of the episcopate. Although the second cannot be envisaged unless it be in direct succession to the first, it remains true that the permanence of Christ's presence is secured by the president of the community who takes the Lord's place. The apostolate, meanwhile, keeps its exceptional role of witness. In this way we see Peter and James jointly direct the Jerusalem council in Acts 15, James (especially in Galatians 2) having a priority over Peter who is even forced to "fear" his representatives. In addition, those two authorities are equally submitted to Truth, of which Paul made himself the mouthpiece right in the middle of the assembly (*emprosthen pantōn,* Gal. 2:14).

The preceding remarks led us to insist, in our interpretation of the New Testament texts, on the importance of the local eucharistic assembly in primitive ecclesiology as the real manifestation of the whole Body of Christ whose image the bishop is. However, the Church very early became conscious of the role of the episcopate as a college to show forth the agreement of all in the faith expressed by Peter on the way to Caesarea. This episcopate is "one" in virtue of the identity of faith in all the local churches, and the throne of each bishop is the one throne, that of Peter confessing the true faith.[17] It is self-evident that, for Cyprian and, with him, the whole primitive tradition, "Peter's throne" meant the concrete functions held by a bishop in a local church: these functions "made" the bishop, just as genuine apostleship came from a direct and individual choice of the Lord. And canonical tradition, still generally in force in the Orthodox Church nowadays, excludes from councils those bishops who are not invested with concrete pastoral functions in a church.

It has also been shown that, for Irenaeus, apostolic succession is, above all, linked with continuity in true doctrine in a given local church. Following this interpretation there is no opposition between the "personal" interpretation of Matthew 16:18 ("The Church is established on the person of Peter.") and the more usual interpretation of the Fathers who followed Origen[18] in asserting the foundation of the Church on the faith of Peter: if the Church is founded on Peter, the reason is that he confessed the true faith; but the episcopal function consists in proclaiming the Word of truth; therefore, the bishops are, *ex officio,* successors of Peter. Within the episcopal college there is, however, a primate, just as Peter was the first among the Twelve, independently of his exceptional role as president of the Jerusalem church. But that primate cannot hold "the place of God" in the universal Church unless one admits that he alone possesses the fullness of sacramental power over all Christians. One has only to be reminded, on that subject, of the opposition of St. Cyprian to whomever it was[19] who pretended to be the "bishop of bishops." This primate is the "first" among the successors of Peter who are all equal to one another and answerable for their ministry to God alone; he can, therefore, just like his brethren, become unfaithful to Peter's faith in making the community, over which he presides, abandon communion of faith with the other churches. The vocabulary used in the ancient Roman councils, which met regularly during the third and fourth centuries, suggests a devotion to St. Peter and his tomb considered as the origin of the one episcopate common to all.[20]

St. Cyprian's doctrine of the episcopate was in no way a private opinion or one peculiar to Africa. It is clearly implicit in the writings of both Eastern and Western scholars, the majority of whom could not have had the benefit of direct influence from the Bishop of Carthage. The image of the "rock" is associated with the episcopate by St. Ignatius of Antioch.[21] St. Gregory of Nyssa speaks of the power of the keys transmitted by Peter to the bishops.[22] The unknown author of the *Corpus Areopagiticum* (although he had very little inclination toward any institutionalized conception of the Church) must reflect an idea current during the sixth century when he evokes Peter as the prototype of the order of "high priests."[23] The same association between Peter and the episcopate constantly reappears in Byzantine homiletics, canonical, and hagiographic literature without any connection with the schism and without the authors having the slightest polemic or apologetic intention with regard to Rome. For instance, the unpublished letters of Athanasius I, Patriarch of Constantinople (1289–1293, 1303–1310), refer to the Petrine texts, especially John 21, in order to describe the episcopal function.[24] His contemporary, Patriarch John XIII (1315–1319), in a letter to the emperor, declares that he accepted the patriarchal throne only after

Christ had appeared to him as to Peter. "If thou lovest me, Peter, feed my sheep."[25]

These Orthodox Byzantine writers who, from the twelfth century onward, opposed Roman ecclesiology, found their strongest argument in the ecclesiology of Cyprian. A few of them adopted a purely negative polemical attitude and denied the exceptional position of Peter in the Church. But the best theologians—Gregory Palamas, Nilus Cabasilas, Symeon of Thessalonica—experienced no difficulty in incorporating into their sermons and their writings the very words of the Byzantine liturgies which extol the role of Peter. Palamas compares him to Adam, for he was the first to confess the faith which the first man denied by his sin, and he gives him the title of "supreme pastor of the whole Church."[26] As for Nilus Cabasilas, he frankly sets the central problem of Peter's succession:

> Now then, some shall say, is the pope in no way Peter's successor? He is, but *as bishop*. . . . For Peter is an apostle, and the chief of apostles (*exarchos tōn apostolōn*), but the pope is neither an apostle (for the apostles did not ordain other apostles, but pastors and teachers), nor even less the leader of the apostles. Peter is the true teacher of the universe; as for the pope, he is bishop of Rome. Peter may have ordained a bishop in Antioch, another Alexandria, and another elsewhere, but the bishop of Rome does not do it. . . .

He then explains the primacy which the Church accorded the Bishop of Rome through a consensus of the ancient Fathers.[27] This quotation from Cabasilas points out clearly the essential difference between the apostolic ministry and the ministry of bishops, which is characterized by the fullness of grace present in each local church. As a last point, I should like to mention the Orthodox reaction to the Calvinistic confession of Cyril Loukaris at the Council of Jerusalem of 1672: the argument used for the defense of the doctrine of the hiearchy is precisely that of the catholic plenitude of each local church. The bishop must be considered as "really head" because the Christians who make up the local church are really "members."[28]

As was sufficiently shown by the debate over Professor Cullmann's book, the central problem posed today about Matthew 16:18 is that of Peter's succession. It is precisely on that problem that a sacramental ecclesiology can shed some light by coming back to the literal and original meaning of the word *ekklesia,* concrete eucharistic community, manifesting the total Christ, Head and members.

NOTES

[1] *Saint Pierre, disciple, apôtre, martyr,* Neuchâtel-Paris, 1953; English translation, second revised edition, *Peter, Disciple, Apostle, Martyr,* Philadelphia, 1962.

[2] See, for example, his *Early Christian Worship,* Naperville, Illinois, 1956.

[3] E. Brunner considers that the origin of a hierarchical Church (betraying, according to him, the New Testament *ekklesia*) lies precisely in the appearance of the sacraments (*The Misunderstanding of the Church,* London 1952, pp. 74 ff.); consequently, one must, of necessity, admit the hierarchy as an integral part of the New Testament doctrine of the Church, if one admits the sacraments.

[4] Cullmann, *La Tradition,* Delachaux-Niestle, 1953.

[5] Such is the opinion of N. Afanassiev in *The Last Supper* (in Russian), Paris, 1959, pp. 9–19.

[6] See A. Schmemann's article on the same problem in relation to ecumenism: "Unity, Division, Reunion in the Light of Orthodox Ecclesiology," *Theologia* XXII, Athens, 1951.

[7] *Epistle to the Smyrnaeans,* VIII:2.

[8] This applies to the Twelve as well as to the itinerant missionaries, also called "apostles." The Didache explicitly says about

them: "Welcome every apostle on arriving as if he were the Lord. But he must not stay beyond one day. In case of necessity, however, the next day too. If he stays three days, he is a false prophet" (XI: 4–5). Timothy and Titus most certainly belonged to this category of itinerant missionaries, although the Didache's time limit was not universally applied.

[9] See J. Colson, *L'évêque dans les communautés primitives,* Collection *Unam Sanctam,* n° 21, Paris, 1951.

[10] Magnesians VI:1; Trallians II; III: 1–2.

[11] *Adversus haereses,* III:3.

[12] *Adv. Haer.* IV:21–22.

[13] On this very point, "the categories of infallibility and error" must be applied to the sacraments, and this is what Cullmann refuses to do, although he admits that "the sacrament is the actualization of the work of Christ" (*La Tradition,* pp. 36–37). But is not the preaching of truth an aspect of that actualization? That truth is always "apostolic," that is, founded only on the apostles' witness, precisely because, "for the sacrament, because of its very nature, there is no difference between the time of the apostles and that of the Church" (*ibid.,* p. 37). The Church, as a sacramental community, is the guardian of the apostolic truth; the one who takes the place of Christ within that community proclaims it and, in doing so, is the successor of the apostles. Moreover, episcopal preaching consists mainly of commenting on apostolic writings.

[14] This fact is perhaps explicitly indicated in the book of Acts if, as is thought by Afanassiev, for instance (*op. cit.,* pp. 9–14), the expression *pantes homɔu epi to auto* (Acts 1:15; 2:1; 3:44; etc.)–literally, "all together at the same thing"—already constitutes a technical term to designate the eucharistic assembly. With Clement (Corinthians 34:7) and Ignatius of Antioch (Ephesians 5:3; Magnesians 7:1) *epi to auto* certainly has that meaning. Fr. Camelot translated it *"réunion commune"* (*Sources Chretiennes,* n° 10, Paris, 1944, p. 53). This interpretation is certainly confirmed by the two possible readings of Acts 2:47 *in fine:* "The Lord, every day, added those who were saved to the same thing" (*epi to auto*) or to the Church (*te ekklesia*). The second variant, which is probably of a later date, could be an interpretation of a copyist who would consider both expressions as synonymous.

[15] Cullmann, *Peter, Disciple, Apostle, Martyr.*

[16] *Cf.,* in particular, Pierre Bonnard, *L'Evangile selon saint Matthieu,* Neuchâtel, 1963, p. 245.

[17] It is impossible here to go into the very complex problem of St. Cyprian's ecclesiology. In any case, it is obvious that the famous fourth chapter of *De Catholicae Ecclesiae Unitate* (in which the Bishop of Carthage develops the doctrine of the *cathedra una,* which is also the *cathedra Petri*) cannot apply solely to Rome; for Rome is no more mentioned than it is in the "parallel passages" in St. Cyprian's work where he speaks of the foundation of the Church on Peter (see A. d'Alès, *La Théologie de saint Cyprien,* Paris, 1922, pp. 121–122). The only exceptions are the letters to the popes Cornelius and Stephen. In the first instance, Cyprian applies to the Church of Rome the title of *cathedra Petri,* of *ecclesia principalis unde unitas sacerdotalis exorta est* ("the principal Church whence came the priestly unity"); here (Ep. 59:14) he is probably speaking of the chronological anteriority of the Roman Christendom in the West without excluding the particular authority this entails (*cf.* de Labriolle in his preface to St. Cyprian's *De Unitate,* collection *Unam Sanctam,* n° 9, Paris, 1942, p. xxvii). In the second instance, Cyprian accuses Stephen of being unfaithful to the faith of Peter: *de episcopatus sui loco gloriatur et se successionem Petri tenere contendit, super quem fundamenta ecclesiae collocata sunt* multas alias petras *inducat* et ecclesiarum multarum *nova aedificia constituat* ("He glories in the place where he enjoys the episcopate and claims Peter's succession on which are laid the Church's foundations and, in so doing, he introduces many new stones [*petras*] and pretends that the multitude of Churches are new constructions" (Ep. 75:17)—since they would not have Peter for foundation.—*J.M.*

[18] "If you think that the whole Church is built only on that one Peter, what shall you say about John, the son of thunder, or about each one of the apostles? Shall we dare to say that the gates of hell will not prevail against Peter personally while they will prevail against the other apostles and the perfect ones? . . . Have the keys of the Kingdom of Heaven been given to Peter alone, and shall no other blessed one receive them? All those who imitate Christ receive their name from the stone [Peter] . . ."—*In Mt.* 12:10; Klostermann, ed., Leipzig, 1935, pp. 85–89 (PG. XIII:997). For the patristic exegesis of the Petrine passages, see also J. Ludwig, *Die Primatwörte Mt. 16, 18, 19 in der altkirchlichen Exegese,* Münster, Westp., 1952.

[19] He not only addresses this reproach to Pope Stephen, but also to an unknown character, Florentius, who wanted to judge the bishops (Ep. LXVI: 3).

[20] *"Cum in unum plurimi fratres convenissemus ad sancti Petri apostoli reliquias per quem et apostolatus et episcopatus in Christo coepit exordium."* "We met together, many brothers, at the tomb of the apostle St. Peter, through whose instrumentality both apostleship and episcopate go back to their origin in fact.") proclaims the Council of 386; *cf.* M. Marot, "Les conciles romains des IVe et Ve siècles," in *L'Eglise et les églises,* I, Chèvetogne, 1954, p. 213.

[21] *To Polycarp* I:1.

[22] *De Castigatione,* PG. XLVI, 312 C.

[23] *Eccl. hier.* VII: 7, PG, III, 564 C.

[24] *Letter to Andronicus* II, Vat. gr. 2219, fol. 41 v.; *Letter to the Bishops, ibid.,* fol. 122 v.; *Letter to the Metropolitan of Apamea, ibid.,* fol. 128; *Instructions to the Bishops, ibid.,* 133 v., 154; *Encyclical, ibid.,* fol. 187 v.; *Letter to Mount Athos, ibid.,* fol. 266.

[25] Pachimeres, *De Andronico Pal.* V:6, ed. Bonn, II, 381.

[26] P(atrologia) G(raeca), CLI, col. 357 A, 360 C.

[27] PG, CXLIX, 704 CD. It is interesting to note the literal concordance between that fourteenth-century Byzantine text and certain passages by Oscar Cullmann: "The function of bishop which is transmissible is essentially different from that of the apostle which is not. The apostles institute bishops, but they cannot bequeathe on them their function which cannot be repeated. . . . They succeed to them, but precisely not as apostles, but *as bishops,* which is an important function in the Church, and a clearly distinct one. . . ." (Cullmann, *La Tradition,* p. 32). For a more detailed study of the Byzantine texts, see our study, "St. Peter in Byzantine Theology" in the collection, *The Primacy of Peter in the Orthodox Church,* (London, Faith Press, 1963).

[28] I. N. Karmires, *Ta dogmatika kai symvolika mnemeia tes Orthodoxou Katholikes Ekklesias,* II, Athens, 1953, p. 752.

2

Ecclesiastical Organization in the History of Orthodoxy

The New Testament writings clearly give no precise definition of the internal organization of the Christian community. Moreover, this community was in existence before the New Testament accounts were written and had a great influence on them. *All* systems of church administration are, therefore, the outcome of a certain interpretation of the Bible, or, rather, of the ecclesiological conception presupposed by the Bible.

"Let all things be done decently and in order," wrote St. Paul to the Corinthians (1 Corinthians 14:40). What is the criterion for defining this "order" (*taxis*) recommended by the Apostle? In St. Paul's view, this criterion is none other than the particular nature of each local community within which the Spirit permanently manifests the will of God. The community obeys "the law of the Spirit" (Romans 8:2) and is the "body fitly joined together and compacted" which "maketh increase of the body unto the edifying of itself in love" (Ephesians 4:16). "In every church" the Apostles "ordained elders" (Acts 14:23, etc.) who formed an essential element in the order of the Church.

The Christian gathering over which these "elders" were called to preside was essentially sacramental in nature. By that we mean that the men who formed it (inasmuch as they had received baptism) really did make up the Body of Christ, the family of God, a holy people of kings and sacrificers (1 Peter 2:5; Revelation 1:6; 5:10; *cf.* Exod. 19:6). The center of their common life was their meeting; "where two or three are gathered together in my name, there am I in the midst of them" (Matthew 18:20). Within this meeting the Christians formed *the same community* as that which met in the upper room, presided over by Christ himself. The man who presides over the Christian gathering is, therefore, the image of Jesus himself.

This inner logical and ritual ecclesiological necessity made the whole Church accept without question and in the very beginning of its existence what is called today "the episcopate": a single head within each community surrounded by "elders," as the "senate" of the apostles surrounded Christ (*cf.* St. Ignatius of Antioch). Ever since the end of the first century, episcopal system has unanimously been accepted by the Church, and the ecclesiological foundation of this institution points to the extreme probability of its apostolic origin: the eucharistic gathering never had more than one president.

THE BISHOP AND THE CHRISTIAN COMMUNITY DURING THE FIRST CENTURIES

Through its meaning and origin, the episcopal ministry is bound up with the local community. The bishop is not an apostle, but the minister who, through the apostles, has received a special *charisma* to preside over the community. His essential functions are not of a missionary order (like those of the apostles), but are sacramental and pastoral. He is not only a "symbol" of Christ. Through him the presence of the Head is just as real as the presence of the Body is real in the community. "I beseech you," writes Ignatius of Antioch about the year 100, "seek to do all things in divine harmony, *under the presidency of the Bishop, who has the place of God at your meeting*" (Magn. VI).

Every Christian community (every "parish," as we should say today) was originally presided over by a bishop elected by that community and consecrated by the bishops of the neighboring communities. He therefore did not exercise his authority *upon* the Church, but *within* the Church. The "apostolic succession" itself did not belong to him as an individual, but was transmitted to him by the apostolic Church to announce the faith of the apostles in his own community which had elected him. The bishop was thus both "the man of his church," which he represented at the councils, and the link uniting his church to all the other Christian communities, many of which were represented at his consecration by their bishops.

Within his church the bishop is, therefore, the high-Priest, the teacher and the shepherd. These three functions are based on the fact that the only High-Priest, the only Teacher and the only Shepherd of Christians is Christ himself and that the Church is really his Body. To be the head of the Body is not a human ministry, but the ministry of Christ; but within the Church the ministries of Christ are accomplished by men, receiving the gifts of the Spirit. Of course, like any other man, the bishop may be unworthy of the *charisma* he has received, and the community is there to control him and correct him, if necessary. The "certain charisma of truth" possessed by the bishops, of which St. Irenaeus of Lyons speaks in the second century (*Adv. Haer.* IV, 40, 2) is not a personal infallibility, but a confirmation of the fact that in the Church everything occurs within the sacramental setting of the eucharistic assembly whose president is the image of our Lord himself. A bishop who is a heretic not only ceases to be a teacher, but also loses the position which he occupied within the Church; since he is no longer the spokesman of Christ, he can no longer occupy "God's place" as high-priest and shepherd. The ministry of the sacrament is not a magic power transmitted to individuals, but an ecclesiastical function involving other obligations, particularly that of preaching the truth.

In the early Church there were thus many cases when bishops were deposed as the result of protests from the congregation (Paul of Samosata). The question has also often been asked whether a bishop, who had been a heretic and had then returned to orthodoxy, could be restored to his see. Church practice varied greatly on this point. It is important, I think, to emphasise these points today when the questions relating to the "apostolic succession" are being widely debated. The Church has never regarded this succession as a reality independent of the life of the Church as a whole and independent of the community within which the episcopal ministry is exercised.

The local churches were in close touch with one another. Their unity was based essentially on *the unity of faith*. "All who wish to see the truth can contemplate the tradition of the Apostles manifested throughout the world in every Church" (Irenaeus, *Adv. Haereses* III, 3, 1). The grace of God, equally present in all the churches, reveals the *same* apostolic truth in *every* church. Any decision or declaration made by one of these churches, if it is made in Christ, must *necessarily* be accepted by all the others or rejected if it is not in accordance with the tradition. There is, therefore, no question here of a democratic "vote," but of the Church witnessing to the Spirit of Truth. No institutional criterion, except the Spirit itself, can define the apostolic tradition and the "charisma of truth" of every bishop within his Church. The mutual agreement between the churches is, therefore, a *sign* given by God in favor of His Church sooner or later—sometimes after long struggles about dogma.

The first three centuries of the Church's history brought some notable changes which were important later on in the organization of the Church. In the first place, the growth in the number of Christians made it essential to increase the number of episcopal communities. Thus, in the third century, there were a great many episcopal sees in the African church. In Asia Minor and other places a different system was adopted; the bishops in the big towns sent elders to minister to the new communities; much more, they deprived the old "country-bishops" of their episcopal rights and reduced them to the status of parish priests. Thus the bishop found himself at the head of several communities or parishes.

Moreover, a certain hierarchy began to arise among the episcopal communities themselves. As far as their sacramental and pastoral functions were concerned, the bishops remained essentially equal, but their communities were not all of equal importance. From the very beginning, the Church in Jerusalem thus had exceptional authority. Later on, "the very large church, very old and universally known, founded in Rome by the glorious Apostles Peter and Paul" (Irenaeus, *ibid.*, III, 3, 2), acquired special importance. Other churches, especially in the East, had greater influence when a decision had to be taken as to whether a certain doctrine should be accepted or rejected, whether a doubtful episcopal election should be confirmed or declared void, or how order should be restored in a community. This exceptional authority was acquired by the churches on different scores. The apostolic basis was particularly venerated in the West, and Rome was the only church which could boast of it. In the East a great many communities were "apostolic" without question; apostolicity alone, therefore, did not bestow any special authority. Numerical importance and seniority, on the other hand, were the preponderant elements. Thus, toward the end of the third century, Rome, Alexandria, Antioch and, to a lesser degree, Carthage possessed exceptional influence in the Christian world. They were four of the most important cities in the Roman Empire.

The authority enjoyed by these churches was not a juridical power which the other churches were to obey; a power of that kind could not have been reconciled with the ontological equality of all the communities. Their authority was a *fact* based on the real influence which they exercised. No decision could be considered definite until they had pronounced their opinion.

Side by side with these big churches of universal influence, all over the Christian world the most important communities possessed an authority greater than that of the small churches, which were often materially dependent and founded by missions from the cities. The bishop from the city was regularly invited to the episcopal consecrations in the district and was the first person who was asked to give his opinion on controversial questions. The Christian Church was confronted by this state of affairs when it was suddenly recognized at the beginning of the fourth century by its former persecutors, the Roman Emperors.

THE CHRISTIAN EMPIRE AND THE ECUMENICAL COUNCILS

As Eusebius, the Church historian, tells us (*De Vita Const.* III:6), the idea of an ecumenical council which would solve the Arian conflict was born in the mind of the Emperor Constantine himself. He had hoped the Church would provide a united religious basis for the Roman Empire, but he found himself confronted by a Christian world which was divided on the question of the divinity of Christ. Determined to put an end to this quarrel, Constantine had recourse to an expedient which was perfectly logical and in accordance with the Church tradition of the local councils: an assembly of all the men who possessed a teaching function in the Church. At the time, therefore, the Council of Nicaea had a value which was both ecclesiastical and political, and so had the ecumenical councils which succeeded it. The faith defined by these councils, which were always convened and often presided over by the Emperors, was regarded by the State as the official faith, and coercive measures were taken (in the name of the State) against those who opposed the councils. The decisions of the councils were included in the official records of Roman law.

However, the Emperors soon realized that their desire (perfectly justified on the political plane) to create a universal ecclesiastical authority which was legally compulsory for all was derisory. Instead of putting an end to the quarrel, the Council of Nicaea became but one of that quarrel's first stages. Arianism soon became so strong that Constantine himself and several of his successors were led to rescind Nicaea. The final triumph of Orthodoxy was brought about much later by the indefatigable struggle of its defendants, Athanasius of Alexandria and the Cappadocian Fathers, and not by the legal decision of a council. The enormous prestige of the Council of Nicaea is due, therefore, to the fact that the Church admitted it afterwards as the faithful expression of the true apostolic doctrine. A Christian historian must recognize here the sovereign will of God who is true to his Church and independent of all human authority. For Nicaea could have been rejected and forgotten just as easily as many Arian episcopal assemblies of the fourth century, as the (Monophysite) Council of Ephesus was in 449 and the unionist assembly in Florence in 1439, all of which fulfilled the criteria generally admitted for the composition of an ecumenical council. The ecumenical councils were, therefore, instituted by the Empire, but the Church turned them into an adequate expression of its doctrine, subject not to the law of the State, but solely to the power of the Spirit.

On the plane of Church organization the ecumenical councils have clearly played an important role. Nicaea proclaimed a general principle which was to determine the later structure of the Church: the administration of the Church will have to conform with the civil circumscriptions defined by the State. This principle, defined by the Nicaean Fathers for obvious reasons of convenience, opened the way to a political-ecclesiastical parallelism whose effects will last throughout the Middle Ages. Very important exceptions were nevertheless admitted by Canons 5 and 6 of Nicaea in favor of those churches which enjoyed special prestige: Rome, Alexandria, Antioch, Jerusalem, and a few others. By referring explicitly to the "old customs," the Council aimed at safeguarding the special "privileges" of these churches and recognized their authority to be wider than the political districts in which they were geographically situated.

METROPOLITANS AND PATRIARCHS

The traditional regulation which laid down that the consecration of any bishop should be effected by several neighboring bishops naturally resulted in the formation of a local council in every civil province. It met originally for consecrations, but soon developed into a permanent institution, it being stipulated in the old canons that it should meet twice a year. (This was the origin of the "synods" of our autocephalous modern churches, which have sole authority to decide on the consecration of bishops.) The bishop of the most important city in the district became its president. From the beginning, the bishops of smaller communities were particularly anxious to receive recognition from this primate. Later on, the councils prescribed that all the episcopal elections should be necessarily recognized by him. The bishop of the main city, or "metropolitan," thus became the head of an ecclesiastical district. Nowadays, in the Greek churches, all bishops are called "metropolitans" if they govern a diocese (the "bishops" with titular dioceses are only assistant bishops) . In Russia and in some Balkan churches the title of "metropolitan" is still reserved to a few main sees.

The decision of Nicaea, which inaugurated the parallelism between the civil and ecclesiastic adminisrations, meant that the ecclesiastical district coincided with the civil province, or "eparchy." The capital of the eparchy thus became automatically the seat of the metropolitan. Nevertheless, in certain provinces "the old customs" were safeguarded and the metropolitans continued to live in a different town from the civil governor of the province (in

Cyprus, for instance). The Roman Church, thanks to its exceptional prestige, continued, as in the past, to exercise "metropolitan" rights over a district much larger than a single eparchy. Ecclesiastical centralism was also safeguarded in Egypt; the "pope" of Alexandria succeeded in checking the schism of Meletius which tended to set up metropolitan districts; he himself continued to control the bishops of the six Egyptian eparchies, that is, the bishops of the whole civil "diocese" of Egypt. The Bishop of Jerusalem, although he was administratively subject to the Metropolitan of Caesarea in Palestine, continued to enjoy an "honorary privilege." The Council recognized that the Church at Antioch had exceptional authority in all the eparchies of the "Eastern diocese."

The legislation of Nicaea therefore had no "patriarchate" yet; the only standard which it recognized was the ecclesiatical province which coincided with the boundaries of a civil eparchy, within which the bishop of the "metropolis" enjoyed a legal primacy. Any deviation from this was an exception, due to the special position of certain churches before the fourth century. This exceptional position in itself did not give them any "rights" apart from those granted by the Council.

It was only later, in the fifth and sixth centuries, that the "patriarchal" regime began to be introduced in the Church. It consisted mainly in extending a little further the parallelism between the organization of the State and the administration of the Church. The Council of Nicaea had decreed that the metropolitans had rights of primacy. Rights of higher primacy were now granted to some bishops on the level of the civil dioceses. Rome even acquired this right progressively over all the dioceses in the West. Alexandria and Antioch, following Nicaea, practically possessed similar rights already over the dioceses in Egypt and the East. Finally the "Patriarchate" of Constantinople was created for the dioceses of Pontus, Asia and Thrace, that is, for Asia Minor and the southeastern part of the Balkan peninsula.

The patriarchal power consisted in the right of appeal, the right of annulment, and sometimes the right of intervention in the internal affairs of the metropolitan provinces. Except in Egypt, where there were no metropolitans, the Patriarch, therefore, did not yet confirm all the episcopal elections, but only those of the metropolitans.

THE TWO ROMES: THE PATRIARCHATE OF CONSTANTINOPLE

Already before Nicaea, the Church at Rome enjoyed a special prestige in the Christian world. As we have already said, it was not a question of one church having "power" over the others, but of a real "authority" justified not only by the fact that the Church of Rome was founded by the apostles, but also by its seniority, its numerical importance, and the incomparable prestige of the capital. None of these elements in itself was enough to give the Bishop of Rome special authority, but altogether they gave him a quite exceptional position. As for the church of the new capital of the Roman Empire, it took its place among the great churches of Christendom through another "fact": the real influence of the Bishop of Constantinople thanks to his direct, permanent access to the Emperor.

This priority given to Constantinople could not be regarded by contemporaries as a caesaropapist revolution, as Roman Catholic historians later asserted. It showed only that it was possible for *any Church* to play a primary role in Christendom, provided that the other churches recognized that its authority was justified.

The Second Ecumenical Council (381), which met at Constantinople, gave an official form to this special role of bishop of the new capital: "The Bishop of Constantinople has the priority of honor after the Bishop of Rome, because Constantinople is a New Rome" (Canon 3). Thus the capital was not recognized as having any special *right,* but simply as having "priority of honor," with special authority (but not power) in the affairs of the Church. The increasing importance of Constantinople was not in competition with the Bishop of Ancient Rome, whose primacy was uncontested; it was directed against Alexandria which still claimed to be second in importance to Rome both in civil and in ecclesiastical affairs.

Nevertheless, a process was taking place for Constantinople which we have already observed in the case of Alexandria and Antioch: their actual authority was progressively transformed into a legal authority which the councils finally declared official, thus giving Constantinople a legally permanent status among the other "patriarchates." The "authority" recognized in the year 381 was manifested in Constantinople's frequent intervention in the ecclesiastical affairs of the three civil dioceses of Thrace, Asia, and Pontus. St. John Chrysostom was one of the most active promoters of these interventions. Finally, the Council of Chalcedon (451) defined the legal setting of Constantinople's authority; like Rome, Alexandria and Antioch, its authority would be exercised over several dioceses; the bishop of the capital would confirm the episcopal elections of the metropolitans in all these territories (Canon 28). This power was defined by the parallelism between the two Romes: "rightly esteeming that the city honored with the presence of the Emperor and the Senate and enjoying the (civil) prerogatives equal to those of ancient imperial Rome, (we agree with the Fathers of the year 381 that the

New Rome) should also enjoy higher rank in ecclesiastical affairs, being second to it in rank."

The ecclesiology which lies behind this text of Chalcedon is perfectly clear: all the churches were equal among themselves; priority could be determined only if it were based on the actual authority possessed by certain churches. Thus, Rome held the first place and enjoyed certain corresponding rights. Constantinople also ought to enjoy similar rights based on the already existing authority conferred on it through the presence of the Emperor.

St. Leo, Pope of Rome, refused to recognize this Canon 28 of Chalcedon. However, it is interesting to note that the texts which contain his protest insist less on the rights of Rome than on those of Alexandria and Antioch which were recognized at Nicaea. Leo seems then to admit that the "privileges" of authority have no compulsory character unless they are formally defined by councils: his main point of reference is Nicaea, and not the "rights" of Rome.

Canons 9 and 17 of Chalcedon recognized Constantinople's right to receive appeals and to re-judge ecclesiastical disputes; this was again a parallel with Rome in favor of which the Council of Sardica had declared similar rights. Finally, in the sixth century, the bishop of the capital took the title of "Ecumenical Patriarch." This title did not suppress the primacy of Rome any more than his other rights; it emphasized only the political basis for his privileges which were closely connected with those of the head of the Christian *Oikoumene,* the Christian Emperor of Constantinople. The title "ecumenical" was thus given not only to "pan-imperial" councils, but also to certain officials in the capital, for instance the ecumenical "master" who was head of the University of Constantinople.

Thus in the fifth century we see the so-called "pentarchy" system firmly established in the Christian world: five "patriarchs" divided the *Oikoumene* among them, and at the time of Justinian they were compared to the "five senses" of the Empire. Their respective rights were similar, but they all recognized the "primacy of honor" and the exceptional authority of Rome. In the East, however, this authority never became absolute; the possibility was unanimously admitted that a pope might fall into heresy. Accordingly, the Sixth Ecumenical Council (681) had no scruple in condemning the memory of Pope Honorius who had supported, though quite involuntarily, the Monothelite heresy.

THE SCHISM

Most of the difficulties which arose between Rome and Constantinople in the ninth and eleventh centuries appear very unimportant to us today. One may feel surprised that such differences could have provoked the greatest scandal known to Christendom. But behind these difficulties lay a deep difference, which very few people realized at the time (except, perhaps, the great patriarch Photius): the two halves of the Christian world had different conceptions concerning *the way to solve the difficulties.* For the West, Rome was the ultimate criterion and the supreme judge; the East remained loyal to a "conciliary" conception of the Church, while recognizing the primacy of Rome and its exceptional, though informal, authority in ecclesiastical affairs.

The works of the Catholic scholar, F. Dvornik, have recently thrown fresh light on the events of the ninth century. Nicholas I, an authoritarian pope who reformed and centralized the Western Church, resolved to extend his reforms to the East, taking advantage of the many appeals addressed to him by the different parts of the Byzantine

Church during their own internal struggles. These appeals were traditional and show that the Eastern Church had not, at the time of Photius, lost its respect for the first See of Christendom whose arbitration was occasionally requested in conformity with the Canons of Sardica in order to solve the internal conflicts of the other churches. Nevertheless Nicholas I's methods finally alienated the two Byzantine parties from him.

The situation was further complicated by a serious doctrinal question. Hitherto the Roman See had been formally opposed to the practice of singing the Creed of Nicaea-Constantinople (a practice which was customary in Spain, Gaul, and the Empire of Charlemagne) with the addition of the *Filioque*. The popes did not succeed in putting a stop to this practice, but the fact that they opposed it in principle gave the Byzantines confidence and led them to hope that one day the West would follow the great Roman Church and would abandon the *Filioque*. The policy of Nicholas I led the Roman Church to support a mission in Bulgaria which competed with that of the Byzantines; the mission was composed of Germanic priests who taught the Bulgarians a version of the Creed which contained the famous addition. By so doing, Nicholas I ruined the reputation for orthodoxy which the Roman See still enjoyed in the East.

In the year 867, Photius, Patriarch of Constantinople, solemnly declared that the Pope was deposed. Photius was compelled almost immediately to abandon his See in a Byzantine internal upheaval. He became Patriarch again in 877 and effected a reconciliation with Pope John VIII by imposing his own conditions: he obtained from the Roman legates an implicit condemnation of the *Filioque* while recognizing Rome's rights of jurisdiction over Bulgaria. The Council of Constantinople (held 879-880), at which this important agreement was concluded, may therefore be regarded as a precedent for a union of churches on an orthodox basis: dogmatic unity defined by a council, and recognition of the canonic primacy of the Roman See. The way in which Photius eulogized John VIII at the end of his own life ought to stimulate the Orthodox to revere the memory of this pope who brought about the reunion of the Christian world.

We do not know the exact date of the final rupture between Rome and Constantinople. It certainly occurred at the beginning of the eleventh century when the Germanic emperors finally imposed the *Filioque* on the Roman Church itself, which was then in a complete state of decadence.

The events of 1054, which are usually regarded as the rupture itself, were really an unsuccessful attempt to reach an agreement, initiated by the Byzantine Emperor. The reasons why it failed are instructive. The main reason was the absence of a common criterion for settling the difficulties. Patriarch Michael Cerullarios, with a certain characteristic brutality, had unified the liturgy within his diocese of Constantinople (where there were a large number of Latin churches) and throughout his partriarchate. This led him to criticise certain usages in the Latin Church. This attitude was just what the Pope of Rome found inadmissible: "How canst thou believe that the Lord concealed from St. Peter and his followers the best rite for celebrating the mass . . . ?" he wrote to Cerullarios.

The two halves of Christendom were already speaking a different ecclesiological language. The contempt of the Byzantines for western "barbarism" (which was justified from the human, but not from the Christian point of view), and the phantastic ignorance of the leaders of the

Roman Church (according to Humbert, the Roman legate, the *Filioque* was part of the original text of the Creed!)—none of these "non-theological factors" helped to settle matters.

On the plane of ecclesiastical organization the schism had extremely important practical consequences for the Eastern Church: the primacy of honor and the right of appeal became the exclusive privilege of the Church of Constantinople–the New Rome. Thus the Church testified to its basic doctrine on the ontological identity of the local churches: the primacy is not the proper prerogative of any particular see; it is entrusted to the Church which can exercise it best while remaining loyal to Orthodoxy. However, it is certain that, on the plane of ecclesiastical organization which concerns us here, the loss of an ecclesiastical authority situated outside the political limits of the Empire resulted in linking the ecclesiastical administrative machinery still more closely to the organization of the Byzantine State and, later on, to the national monarchies of the Christian countries in the East.

THE BYZANTINE CHURCH

The events of the tenth and eleventh centuries were hardly perceived in the New Rome which was at the zenith of its political and cultural influence. The Byzantines regarded the West as an essentially barbaric form of Christianity whose theological opinions and ecclesiastical practices were not worth taking really seriously. It was a terrible surprise for the whole of Eastern Christendom, enclosed as it was in its own cultural pride and traditional orthodoxy, when the Crusaders arrived in the East, full of youthful vigor, and turned aside from their original goal to sack "the Queen of Cities." The proud disdain of the Eastern Christians turned into a fierce hatred of the Latins which lasted for many centuries.

During the whole period between the eleventh and fifteenth centuries the Patriarchate of Constantinople was incontestably the center of Orthodoxy. But, as in the past, the Church continued to be governed by the old canons, and the Patriarch never claimed any sort of infallibility or any superior authority upon the decision of the councils. One sometimes wonders why no ecumenical council was held during this period. The reason is quite simple: the concept of the *Oikoumene* was a political idea used to describe the universal Roman Empire of which the Orthodox Emperor of Constantinople continued (legally, at least) to be the head. In principle, this Empire included the West. If he had convened an ecumenical council without the Western churches, this would have implied that the sovereign of Constantinople renounced his own rights to the universal Empire.[1] On two occasions he consented to united councils of this kind, giving them the title of "ecumenical": the councils, held at Lyons (1281) and at Florence (1439), were failures; their only effect was to deepen the schism still further.

However, the absence of ecumenical councils did not mean that the Orthodox Church felt incapable of dealing with the theological controversies or of pronouncing definitions of dogma. It did so on several occasions. For instance, the councils held in 1341, 1347, 1351 and 1368 defined the Orthodox doctrine of grace, and their decisions (which were included in the *Synodikon* of Orthodoxy and in the liturgical books in use throughout the Church) are considered as official Orthodox doctrine. Other examples could be quoted. The Church thus testified that its doctrine is not limited by the decisions of ecumenical councils, and that the definition of this doctrine can and must take place every time this is necessary to safeguard Orthodoxy; for the sole guardian of truth is the Spirit of Truth which is loyal to the Church.

As at the beginning, the Patriarch of Constantinople continued to be the bishop of the capital of the Empire. His power was, therefore, closely connected with that of the emperors. The Byzantine "theocracy" was thus a sort of "diarchy" of the Emperor and the Patriarch, "the two most essential members of the State," as Patriarch Photius says in his *Epanagogé*. It would be erroneous, however, to consider the Byzantine regime as a form of caesaropapism. Even after the separation from Rome, the Church did not pay allegiance to the State. It had concluded what Father Schmemann calls "a dogmatic alliance" with the Empire: the Emperor possessed an authority which was officially recognized for defining the limits of the patriarchates and of the ecclesiastical provinces. He often had the casting vote when Patriarchs were appointed, but he had no power over the canons and dogmas defined by the Church. Thus several emperors incurred excommunication for having infringed the rules of the Church: Leo VI through his fourth marriage; Michael VIII Palaeologus for having betrayed Orthodoxy by joining Rome.

The authority of the Byzantine Patriarch threw into the shade the other Eastern Patriarchs: the Patriarchs of Alexandria, Antioch, and Jerusalem who lived in countries ruled by Islam. However, he never contested their rights.

When Constantinople itself finally fell in 1453 to the Turks, the authority of the Patriarch of New Rome was even reinforced. The new Mohammedan rulers invested him with civil and legal authority over all the Orthodox Christians within the Ottoman Empire for which he became responsible in the eyes of the Turkish Government.

Without modifying his canonical rights, this decision on the part of the Turks gave the Patriarch very extensive power, though it was often controlled by the Government.

THE SLAVIC CHURCHES

One of the glories of Orthodox Byzantine Christianity is its missionary work toward the North. Beginning with the ninth century, several Slavic people were baptized by Greek missionaries and received the cultural heritage of the Christian East. One of the inevitable elements of this heritage was the political system of Byzantium which was intrinsically bound up, throughout the whole of the Middle Ages, with the Orthodox Church and its traditions: the "diarchy" which existed in Constantinople between the Emperor and the Patriarch was the very basis of the "symphony" between Church and State. This system was transplanted, just as it was, into the Slavic states. Nevertheless, the sovereign of Constantinople continued legally to be the universal Emperor, the legitimate heir of Constantine and Justinian. In theory the Byzantine Empire was not a national state, but the universal City of God established on earth. On many occasions the Emperors drew attention solemnly in official documents to their status as sovereigns over *all* Christians. It was only owing to this status that the universal Church had recognized them as protectors and that they convened the ecumenical councils. In practice, however, the Byzantine Empire had become a monolithically Greek state ever since the seventh century. It would be completely erroneous to recognize in the political consciousness of the Byzantines the "national" sentiment as it appeared in secularized Europe after the French Revolution. It is an undeniable fact, however, that the ethnic character of the Byzantine state after the seventh century made the universal mission at which it aimed more delicate.

The new Slavic states, Bulgaria and Serbia, made use of the Byzantine heritage for their own advantage. In their respective capitals they created concurrent "little Byzantiums."[2] When the political and military situation permitted, they even went so far as to claim the universal Orthodox Empire for themselves. In practice, however, they created national churches which led an independent life while recognizing the "primacy of honor" of the Eastern Patriarchs. The Byzantine Patriarch admitted their right to elect their bishops and primates themselves—a right which certain eastern provinces of the Eastern Church, like Cyprus or Georgia, had possessed for some time. But every time the political situation or the fortune of war permitted, Constantinople suppressed the political and ecclesiastical independence which it had only half-heartedly admitted, and re-established the authority of the New Rome in the East. The last time it did so was under the Turkish regime, when the Patriarch was instated by the Sultans as Head of the Orthodox Christians of the Ottoman Empire.

The resentment felt by modern Slavic historians against Byzantium is, therefore, understandable, but it can be only partly justified. They often forget that in the Middle Ages "nationalism" (in the modern sense of the word) was unknown both in the West and in the East. Everyone then admitted in principle the *universality* of Christendom expressed within a single Empire. The "national" independences then constituted a "disorder" which was prejudicial to the Christian cause. The Emperor and the Byzantine Patriarch, therefore, had the moral right to put an end to it. Their policy undeniably favored one nationality at the expense of the others, but this "reverse side of the picture" only illustrated the decadence of the "imperial idea" itself, and this decadence was provoked by the appearance of nationalism.

RUSSIA

The relations of Russia with the Mother-Church of Byzantium were never exactly the same as those of the Slavs in the Balkans. The State of Kiev had become a Christian principality in the tenth century, but it did not enjoy ecclesiastical autonomy until the fifteenth century, although an attempt in this direction had been made right at the beginning of its existence. Being further away from Byzantium, Russia felt the sovereign authority of Constantinople less than Bulgaria or Serbia, and did not rebel against it. The metropolitans of Kiev were, therefore, always nominated by the Byzantine Patriarch and were always Greeks (with a few exceptions).

This system of ecclesiastical administration had deep consequences for the later destiny of Russian Christianity. The Byzantine Church, which was anxious to keep close ecclesiastical control over the immense territories in the North, did not favor the consecration of local bishops of Russian origin. The Greek Metropolitan who lived at Kiev, at Vladimir, and later at Moscow, was really the sole head of an immense diocese and the rights of the Russian clergy under his control were strictly limited. This was the origin of the centralism of the Russian Church which was quite contrary to the ancient canons and to the practice of the Eastern and Balkan Churches.

When, in the thirteenth century, Russia fell under the Mongol yoke, the metropolitans of Kiev, who were still appointed by Constantinople, were true spiritual leaders of the people, independent of the invaders and of the feudal princes.

The ecclesiastical situation was completely changed in Russia in the fourteenth and fifteenth centuries. The Church of Russia was divided into two metropolitan districts: that of Kiev in the Grand-Duchy of Lithuania (which was soon to fuse with the Kingdom of Poland), and that of Moscow. The metropolitan district of Kiev remained attached to the Patriarchate of Constantinople until the seventeenth century. The metropolitan district of Moscow became "autocephalous" in the fifteenth century and was raised to a patriarchate in the sixteenth century.

The Church of Moscow inherited the ecclesiastical centralization instigated by the Byzantine administration. The Patriarch was admitted to the fifth place (after Constantinople, Alexandria, Antioch, and Jerusalem); it thus constituted one of the pillars of the New Empire which claimed to be the heir of the universal Christian Empire—the "Third Rome." But the "symphony" between Church and State (the ideal of Byzantine theocracy) was never realized in Russia. Long before Peter the Great, and contrary to what is generally thought ever since the sixteenth century, the Tsars of Moscow had derived their political ideology from the West rather than from Byzantium. The Middle Ages were over. By becoming independent and by accepting the alliance of the Muscovite State, the Church of Russia had lost the support of the distant Patriarch of Constantinople and was subject to the State to an extent never experienced by the Byzantine Church. Among the Patriarchs there were only a few great characters who succeeded in imposing their will on the State. The most famous, undeniably, was Nikon in the seventeenth century who carried out a reform of the liturgy in Russia in order to bring the Russian practice into conformity with the contemporary Greek practice; he was the real master of Russia for many years.

In order to avoid similar events, Peter the Great suppressed the patriarchate at the beginning of the eighteenth century (thus violating the tradition of the Canons) and replaced it by the "Holy Synod." This institution was modelled closely on the ecclesiastical organisms of Protestant Europe; it was an integral part of the State (parallel to the Senate) and its decisions had to be submitted to the approval of the Tsar. A State official, the "higher-procuror," attended the meetings of the Synod (which was composed of a limited number of bishops and priests), and he was the real head of the synodal administration. This administration accentuated ecclesiastical centralism still more in favor of an anonymous collegiate institution strictly controlled by the State. The bishops in Russia had never been in close touch with their dioceses, which were too vast and too dependent; after Peter the Great they became officials of the synodal administration, frequently transferred, in violation of the Canons, from one see to another.

This state of affairs continued until 1917. From the end of the nineteenth century, public opinion unanimously demanded a reform, and special commissions performed a great deal of work for this purpose. The Church of Russia was, therefore, better equipped to confront the revolution than is often thought. A council, which met in Moscow in 1917 and 1918, thoroughly reformed the administration of the Church by re-establishing the patriarchate, arranging for the Bishops to be elected by the people, and giving the laity opportunities to participate in every aspect of Church life. But the Council did not re-establish in Russia the episcopal community of the early Church: the dioceses remained too vast, and the central administration of the patriarchate (which included some lay representatives) still had the right to encroach upon some of the traditional rights of the local bishops. The reforms of 1917–18 were inspired by the ideal of the *sobornost* and preferred to express it through a "democratic" administration on the national plane rather than to restore the link between the local bishop and his Church. But although these reforms did not restore certain canonical standards of the old Church, they opened the door for their revival.

Circumstances did not permit these decisions to be carried out completely. When the Patriarchate of Moscow reappeared in 1943, these decisions of the Council of 1917 were replaced by an absolute patriarchal autocracy which was quite as severe as that of the Holy Synod. Ecclesiastical administration in Russia today differs, therefore, from that in the East and in the Balkans in two ways. In the first place, the Russian Church has a centralized discipline which places the bishops in close dependence on the Patriarch; he has authority, with the formal approval of a small synod, to transfer them, to reward them with honorary distinctions, or to force them to retire. The second difference in the Russian Church is that it has very few dioceses (only 69 for nearly one hundred million Orthodox Christians, whereas Greece has 81 dioceses for seven million believers) ; the Russian Bishop is therefore a large-scale administrator who has only chance contacts with his flock.

THE MODERN "AUTOCEPHALOUS" CHURCHES

The progressive liberation of the Balkan peninsula from Turkish domination and the appearance of a number of new, independent States, had immediate repercussions in the ecclesiastical realm. For, ever since the Council of Nicaea, the Orthodox Church had adopted the principle of dividing its dioceses so that their frontiers coincided with the political frontiers of the provinces or states.

On the strictly canonical plane, "autocephaly" is the right granted to a diocese or group of dioceses to elect its own bishop or bishops. During the very early days of Christianity every local church was, therefore, autocephalous. Today the autocephalous Archbishop of Sinai is a relic of that old custom. However, as we pointed out above, the authority of the bishops in the large towns (metropolitans), who were regularly called upon to consecrate bishops in less important churches, soon acquired the official right to confirm all the episcopal elections in their province. Even today the fact that the Archbishop of Sinai is consecrated by the Patriarch of Jerusalem gives the latter a certain authority over that ancient autocephalous diocese. Thus autocephaly almost always became the privilege of a province including several dioceses.

Later on, the metropolitans themselves entered the orbit of the five great patriarchates while sometimes remaining autocephalous. Although they were elected on the spot, they regarded themselves as spiritually dependent on a patriarch and admitted his right of appeal and certain rights to intervene on questions of discipline.

Although autocephaly, in the strictly canonical sense, remained a simple right for a province to elect its own bishops, in the nineteenth century it acquired a new sense: it identified itself, at least as far as the Balkans were concerned, with the absolute independence of the new national churches. This psychological evolution was clearly linked up with the appearance of a modern form of nationalism, unknown in the Middle Ages, which always remained true to the ideal of a universal Christian theocracy. The ideologists of the new "autocephalies" were not solely responsible for this; their action was often provoked by the confusion (often admitted by the Phanar) between the interests of Orthodoxy and those of modern Hellenism.

At the beginning of the nineteenth century there were seven autocephalous or autonomous Churches in the Balkans: four of Serbian language (Montenegro, the Patriarchate of Carlovitz, the Archbishopric of Belgrade and the autonomous Church of Bosnia-Herzegovina), two Roumanian-speaking (Roumania and Transylvania), and one Roumano-Serbian (Bukovina). Their boundaries corresponded with the administrative districts of Austria-Hungary and the Turkish Empire. After the first World War, the Archbishop of Belgrade, who had been raised to the rank of Serbian Patriarch (1920), grouped the Serbian Churches around him. In 1925 the Roumanian Churches also united under the Roumanian Patriarch. The case of the Bulgarian Church caused a series of troubles: the negotiations between the Bulgarian representatives and the Ecumenical Patriarch were obstructed by the existence of a large Bulgarian population in Constantinople itself. The Bulgarians claimed that these people were also subject to the authority of the new Bulgarian "autocephaly" as far as ecclesiastical affairs were concerned. A system of this kind would have been an official admission of the existence of two parallel Church hierarchies on the same territory. It was impossible to avoid a rupture: in 1872 the Council of Constantinople officially condemned the primacy of racialism or nationalism in Church affairs. It is interesting to note that the Orthodox Church officially condemned this psychological malady just at the dawn of an epoch in which Orthodoxy all over the world was to suffer as a result of ecclesiastical nationalism. The "Bulgarian schism" was settled in 1945; Bulgarian autocephaly was then established and recognized without any infringement of the "territorial" principle.

It is a regrettable fact, however, that after 1920 the "nationalization" of the Orthodox autocephalies, dispersed in different countries, gave rise to violations of the territorial principle, especially in America, and this violation did considerable harm to the Orthodox message in the world.

In addition to the autocephalies in Serbia, Roumania, and Bulgaria in the nineteenth century, the "Church of Hellade" sprang up in the Kingdom of Greece (1850). In the twentieth century, autocephalous churches finally appeared in Albania, Poland, and Czechoslovakia; no definite solution has yet been found for their canonical position.

THE EASTERN PATRIARCHATES TODAY

In spite of the relatively small number of members, the four ancient Patriarchates of Constantinople, Alexandria, Antioch, and Jerusalem constitute an extremely important symbol for all Orthodox Christians and maintain incontestable authority. This remnant of the old "pentarchy" of the five patriarchs prevents the universal Orthodox Church from becoming a "federation" of national autocephalies organized on overly secularized principles.

The Patriarchate of Constantinople occupies the first place, which formerly belonged to the Church of Rome. By virtue of his authority as primate, the Ecumenical See often had to intervene (like ancient Rome) in Church disputes. Differences of opinion have recently come to light concerning the exact interpretation of this primacy, which is said to be contrary to the equality of the autocephalous "sister-Churches" and to promote a kind of "papism." Some canonical error on the part of Constantinople may have provided a pretext for this opposition. But it is an incontestable fact that the authority of the *primus inter pares* is an integral part of Orthodox ecclesiology and that the present position of the Patriarch of Constantinople—

whom events had placed outside the geographical limits of nationalism—gives him an opportunity to exercise that authority fruitfully.

MONASTICISM

The monasteries have always occupied a special place in the Orthodox Church, while conforming with the essential principles which reflect the nature of the Church.

Monasticism, which appeared in the third and fourth centuries, has always been valuable as a prophetic witness. When the Christians "settled down" in this world under a Roman Empire which was nominally Christian, the monks went off into the desert, saying that it was impossible for the Church to be "reconciled" with the world which will always remain fallen and sinful. When people tended to identify medieval Christianity with "the City of God," the very existence of the monks was a reminder that the City of God will not be established on earth until the last day. In order to carry out this witness, the monks had to form separate communities, and here is the origin of certain "episcopal" characteristics with which the abbots (or *higoumenoi*) of monasteries were invested. However, the Church could not allow its own unity to be disturbed, and the witness of the monks had to remain within the sacramental body of the Church. Hence, Orthodox Canon Law firmly maintains the principle of the submission of the monasteries to the local diocesan bishops. No "monastic orders" have ever appeared in the Orthodox Church such as those in the West which enjoy an "exemption" which makes them directly dependent upon the Pope.

Within the Church the monks formed a spiritual elite which exercised tremendous influence on the life of the Church as a whole. In the sixth century the Canon Law stipulated that the episcopacy must be drawn from the monastic body; this law is still valid today.

CONCLUSION

The Orthodox Church, even today, has no exhaustive canon law comparable with the *Corpus juris canonici* of the Roman Church. The councils have never claimed to compose any document of this kind, and the *Nomocanan* itself (a Byzantine collection of canonical and legislative texts concerning ecclesiastical life) merely summarized and classified the few rules which had almost all been enacted by the Church authority in order to settle certain definite cases. It is, therefore, not surprising that there should be disagreements about the canon law in the Orthodox Church right up to the present time and that these old laws should be interpreted in different ways.

Nevertheless, Orthodoxy remains surprisingly faithful to certain basic principles which have ruled the life of the Church since the earliest times. If we try to express these principles, we immediately see that they are not canonical rules in the proper sense; they are, rather, the outcome of a theological conception of the Church which could not possibly be fitted into a juridical frame. The canons have, therefore, no purpose except to indicate how we can remain faithful to the nature of the Church in the different historical circumstances in which we find ourselves.

The Church recognizes that these indications in the Canon are not complete. In certain cases the Church applies the principle of "economy" by infringing the rules when this serves the common good, without modifying the rules themselves. Thus the Church admits that a bishop may change his see, while, at the same time, it maintains the principle that an episcopal election definitely binds the pastor to his church. The application of the principle of "economy" is particularly evident in the different practices which have existed for admitting non-Orthodox: sometimes mere schismatics have been re-baptized, while real heretics have been admitted after a simple penance, just as the Church daily re-admits its own members who have sinned.[3] Indeed, how could the Church have defined (for the purpose of canon law) a fact as contrary to its own nature as the division of Christians? It applied different remedies to the malady of schism, and it is this very diversity in the remedies which can effect the cure.

The application of the principle of "economy" can, however, lead to the greatest abuses when it is confused with the norm itself. The unity of the Church, which is one of the essential elements of its nature, requires that Orthodox Christians, living in the same place, should form a single community and be under the authority of a single bishop. As we have seen above, the defense of this principle was the cause of the "Bulgarian schism" of 1872. But do not the Orthodox, "dispersed" in America or Europe, make a point today of being "non-canonical" and of systematically infringing this principle, without having any "economy" to justify them?

Throughout its history, Orthodoxy has passed through considerable variations in ecclesiastical administration, and it will probably experience still further variations in future, for instance when Christ's will for the unity of all Christians is accomplished in history. But these variations are only justified if they conform with the nature of the Church, with the expression of its unity, holiness, apostolicity, and catholicity.

Within the Christian tradition which grew out of the Reformation, the question of Church administration is usually regarded as secondary. This is not true of Orthodoxy which holds that the normative elements of the ecclesiastical structure are part of the Revelation inasmuch as the Church (in accordance with the will of its Head) is a permanent, living organism existing in history. These norms are not human in origin; they are fixed by the sacramental nature of the Church which assumes an organized community always identical to itself and identical to other communities which are equally faithful to the apostolic message. Being human, we may betray this message; but God does not betray His people, nor does He modify the nature of the redemptive grace which is always present in the Church of God. There have, therefore, been "legitimate" variations in the rules of ecclesiastical administration in history; others were contrary to the nature of the Church. The former were inevitable and helped to strengthen the Christian message or to express it in forms suitable to the historic circumstances of the time (for instance, in face of the existence of a world-wide Christian Empire) ; the others, which were contrary to the nature of the Church, must be overcome (with the help of the Holy Spirit), so that the local church which adopts them may not become unfaithful to its Head.

NOTES

[1] Cf. our study, "Projets de concile oecuménique en 1367: un dialogue inédit entre Jean Cantacuzene et le légat Paul," in *Dumbarton Oaks Papers,* XIV, 1960, pp. 149–177.

[2] A good analysis of this process is to be found in A. Schmemann, *The Historical Road of Eastern Orthodoxy,* New York, 1963.

[3] I. Karmires, "The Ways of Admitting the non-Orthodox in the Church," in *The Greek Orthodox Theological Review,* I, 1954.

3

*The Roman Primacy in Canonical Tradition up to the Council of Chalcedon**

The purpose of this chapter is to give a general outline of an Orthodox approach to the Roman primacy in the ancient Church through the canons of the councils of that period. The ecclesiology underlying those decisions belongs to our common past; studying it could lead to a return to the sources which is necessary for the reunion desired by all. The interest of this theme has been increased by the work of Catholic scholars, and the recent developments within the Church of Rome call for objective dialogue.

The Church of Rome and its place among the other

*Originally published in French in *Istina,* N° 4, pp. 463–482.

episcopal sees are mentioned by the canons of four councils of the first five centuries: Nicaea, (325), Sardica (probably 343), Constantinople (381), and Chalcedon (451). The author does not take into account the hypothesis of P. Battifol who sees an allusion to the Bishop of Rome in Canon 58 of the Council of Elvira held in Spain. As far as he knows, all historians today are agreed in seeing there only an allusion to the greater authority which the bishops of older churches had in Spain.[1] It concerns, therefore, a purely local situation.

As a preliminary to the study of canonical texts, it must be pointed out that no council instituted the Roman primacy which the councils always assumed to be an accepted fact. The clause in Canon 28 of the Council of Chalcedon which asserts that "the Fathers recognized privileges to Old Rome" cannot refer to any particular council, but to the whole pre-Nicene tradition which recognizes for the Church of Rome a special position within the Christian universe. The breach between East and West will take place later; it will happen as the consequence of different interpretations of that tradition. All the conciliary decisions aimed, in principle, at preserving the pre-Nicene heritage by giving it some legal framework, if only a partial one.

It is evident, on the other hand, that the councils of the first five centuries created no exhaustive system dealing with or intending to deal with all possible cases which could arise in the relationships between members of the Church. These councils intended to:

1. Determine some very *general* principles which could give expression to the essential elements of the ecclesiastical structure; such elements are themselves determined by the grace of the Holy Spirit, and not by canonical decisions.

2. Solve *particular* cases endangering that structure.

3. Adapt the principles of that structure to the new circumstances of the post-Constantinian Church.

In consequence, the aim of this study is to determine the *principles* which the councils wanted to defend. According to the same councils, those principles go back to the pre-Nicene Church.

THE SIXTH CANON OF NICAEA

This canon originated in the desire to maintain ancient principles within a new ecclesiastical organization brought about by historical circumstances. It is a known fact that the First Ecumenical Council adopted a general rule which made the organization of the Church coincide with that of the Roman Empire with which the Church had recently concluded a close alliance. For instance, Canon 4 of Nicaea stipulates that bishops must be ordained by their colleagues of the civil province in which the vacant see was situated. Their action must receive confirmation from the bishop of the main provincial city, the metropolitan. Canon 5 regulates the methods of convocation of a provincial council.

Some of these measures confirmed already existing practices. The recognition and the ordination of a new bishop by his colleagues of neighboring churches and, in particular, the confirmation of his election by the bishop of the main church of the area were principles known before Nicaea. The metropolitan's *right* to confirm episcopal elections in his province was the essential novelty introduced by this Council. It gave his authority a legal character.

In addition, when measures adopted at Nicaea were applied, the previously existing situations were taken into account. In most cases, the capital of the civil province was considered as Mother Church and metropolitan see. And, as Christianity had usually spread first to the large cities, these were most frequently the center of the oldest and most famous churches. But the bishops of certain ancient sees continued to be considered as metropolitans even when their city was not the capital of the province. This seems to have been the case for Salamis, the Metropolitan See of Cyprus, which had Paphos as its civil capital.

Canon 6 of Nicaea shows another exception to the general rule which made civil provinces and ecclesiastical connections coincide:

> The ancient customs of Egypt, Lybia, and Pentapolis shall be maintained: the bishop of Alexandria will exercise his power over all these provinces, since that is also the custom of the bishop who is in Rome; similarly in Antioch and in other provinces, the prerogatives of [some] Churches must be preserved. But, in general, it is evident that if someone has become bishop against the wish of the metropolitan, the great council rules that he is not a bishop. However, if two or three, in a spirit of contradiction, challenge the general suffrage after it has taken place correctly and according to ecclesiastical rule, the majority shall prevail.

This canon has been the object of many comments and of conflicting interpretations. It brings out a whole series of problems which do not all concern us directly.[2] This chapter's investigation will be limited to the meaning of the reference to the Roman Church, the nature of the prerogatives recognized by the Council for some Churches, and, finally, the information available about the Nicene Fathers' reasons for recognizing special privileges for some Churches.

1. The text of Canon 6 envisages primarily the ecclesi-

astical situation in Egypt. During the first years of the fourth century there had been an open conflict: on the one hand there were those who favored centralization and wanted to concentrate exclusively into the hands of the Bishop of Alexandria the power of episcopal consecration within the *six* provinces which made up the Roman "diocese" of Egypt; on the other hand there were those who wished to establish in Egypt provincial ecclesiastical districts in which communities would be grouped around local metropolitan sees. Needless to say, the second tendency represented by Meletius, Bishop of Lycopolis, was at least apparently much more traditional, while the desire of the Alexandrian "pope" to concentrate power into his hands was an exception in the Christian world. The Nicene Fathers were obliged to publish in his favor an exceptional legislation because they could not, and they did not, want to diminish the authority of Arius' great adversary, Alexander of Alexandria. In fact, Alexandria's privileges ran contrary to the general principle adopted at Nicaea which recognized each province's ecclesiastical independence. The Council was very conscious of establishing a special order of things in favor of Alexandria, and it tried to preserve tradition elsewhere as far as possible. In particular, the same Canon 6, in its second part, confirmed the general rule excluding interference from any authority other than the provincial council in the affairs of the province.

The Nicene Fathers justify this flagrant exception to the general rule by another guiding principle: not to infringe on the exceptional prerogatives already existing in some Churches. The Bishop of Alexandria's *exousia* (power) is acceptable "since that is also the custom of the Bishop of Rome"; "similarly in Antioch and in other provinces the prerogatives of some Churches must be preserved." Notice that the canon mentions definitely the *personal* privileges of the Bishop of Rome, while the reference to customs allowed "in Antioch and other provinces" is more general. If there were discussions relative to the privileges of Alexandria, it is likely that the Nicene Fathers gave way to the Alexandrine arguments which among others must have called on the principle already enunciated by St. Irenaeus: "*ad hanc ecclesiam necesse est omnem convenire ecclesiam*"—"all Churches must agree with that Church" (*Adv. Haer.* 2), that is, with Rome. The Roman custom which gave to one bishop the power to confirm his colleagues' elections over a territory larger than a secular province[3] was recognized by the Nicene Fathers who allowed the same customs for Alexandria. This witnesses explicitly to the enormous and exceptional authority enjoyed by the Bishop of Rome in the Christian world of the early fourth century.

Catholic historians, however, are often disturbed by this equality proclaimed between Rome and Alexandria by the Council of Nicaea, for, indeed, Rome is referred to as an *example,* not as a source of authority. This equality, according to them, applies only to the patriarchal privileges of the Roman See and not to its universal primacy. It is questionable, however, whether the Fathers of 325 would also have made that distinction. In any case, it was in virtue of the universal Roman primacy that they were able to refer to the *example* of the Roman Church in order to admit the exceptional prerogatives claimed by the Bishop of Alexandria. Their conception of *primacy* rested on the moral *authority* which they recognized in the See of Rome, always making that Church an example and a reference. The Roman customs, without bearing a compulsory legal character, could credit a practice allowed by the Roman Church, not because that Church enjoyed a universal jurisdiction, but because it was the Church "very great, very ancient, known by all, founded and established by the two very glorious apostles Peter and Paul" (Irenaeus, *Adversus haereses,* III:2), and which, as a consequence, enjoyed a *"potentior principalitas" (ibid.).* In brief, there was no legal authority, but a moral one.

2. This interpretation is confirmed by the meaning of the word which is mentioned in this general statement: "similarly in Antioch and in other provinces, the prerogatives [*presbeia*] of the Churches must be preserved." Some sees—Rome, Alexandria, Antioch, and others—enjoyed *privileges* of antiquity, apostolicity, authority, which gave them more authority and which the Council meant to preserve. It achieved that by transforming them into *legal authority.* For example it admits that the *presbeia* which are ancient customs *(archaia ethe)* can materialize into legal power (*exousia*). This power consists essentially in the right to ordain all the bishops within a group of secular provinces.[4]

3. Three Churches are mentioned in Canon 6 as enjoying *presbeia*: Rome, Alexandria, Antioch. A direct analogy is established between the first two. The allusion to Antioch did not pretend to an authority as great as that of Alexandria. Its moral authority, the embryo of the future patriarchate, was exercised over a large number of dioceses, but it does not seem to have been as direct an authority as that of the Alexandrian "pope."[5] Nevertheless, it is clear that the three Churches are isolated by the Nicene Fathers as breaking the structure of normal ecclesiastical organization.

Through what particular merit did these three cities acquire the authority which was now confirmed? Was it because of their apostolicity? This did not seem to be the case, at least as far as Alexandria was concerned. The tradition according to which the Church was established there by St. Mark would have been, by itself, insufficient for the Church of Alexandria to claim privileges similar to those of Rome: a very large number of Eastern Churches could claim a much more impressive apostolic foundation accredited by New Testament writings. In particular, this was the case for Antioch which was content with the third place, after Rome and Alexandria. Moreover—and this has been pointed out several times by historians—a Church's apostolic origin was a far too common factor in the East to have had the importance it acquired in the West where the Roman See was the only apostolic see and the main center from which evangelization spread.[6] The Egyptian pontiff, in particular, never claimed an apostolicity which was in any case doubtful, even when, after the First Council of Constantinople in 381, he had to defend himself against the bishop of the capital of the empire. The fifth-century popes eventually drew attention to Alexandria's apostolicity by giving it a Petrine foundation: a disciple of Peter had founded that Church, and Peter himself had been Bishop of Antioch before coming to Rome. This theory, propounded by the famous *Decretum Gelasianum,* is manifestly artificial and does not explain Alexandria's preponderence over Antioch. It never found echo in the East, even in circles which could have been interested in lowering Constantinople's prestige.

Without excluding the idea of apostolicity, which may have played some role in the elevation of Alexandria and Antioch, the full explanation of the sixth Nicene canon must be sought elsewhere. The original text gives us no indication. However, it is interesting to mention a Latin version of the sixth canon which spread in Italy, that of the manuscript of Chieti. It reads as follows: "*Ecclesia*

Romana semper habuit primatum. Teneat autem et Egyptus, ut episcopus Alexandriae omnium habeat potestatem, quoniam et Romano episcopo haec est consuetudo. Similiter autem et qui Antiochia constitutus est, et in ceteris provinciis primatus habeant ecclesiae civitatum ampliorum"[7] ("The Roman Church always possessed the primacy. Egypt must also preserve the custom according to which the Bishop of Alexandria also possesses a supreme authority since the Bishop of Rome enjoys the same responsibilities. The same must hold for the bishop established in Antioch, and let the *most important cities* in other provinces enjoy the primacy.").

This Latin paraphrase, while it underlines strongly the Roman primacy, gives the importance of cities as the obvious explanation for all the primacies created by the Council after the Roman model. It proves at least the existence and the relative popularity of that interpretation in the fourth century even in the West.[8]

Without question, Alexandria was the first city of the East during the whole pre-Constantinian period. One needs only to mention the Christian *Didascaleion* which could justify, all by itself, the prestige of the Christian community of Alexandria. As for Antioch, the Jewish historian Josephus speaks about it as the Church "possessing the third place":[9] the analogy with the Nicene canon is flagrant.

Yet this does not mean that we want to see the size of cities as the only element determining the hierarchy of future patriarchal sees: it was, above all, the *authority* and *prestige* acquired by Christian communities which determined their position. That prestige was made up partly of those Churches' apostolicity. But did not the apostles themselves direct their evangelization primarily toward the larger cities of the Empire where ideologies were in competition and where a favorable field for preaching could be found in the important Jewish communities? Thus the Roman Church was able to unite the various elements which fully justified its primacy of authority. Situated in the Empire's first city which had attracted the apostles Peter and Paul, the Roman Church acquired a very particular claim to apostolicity. Its numerical importance, its central position, and, above all, the unshakeable orthodoxy of its bishops justified its primacy. These various elements are reflected, in particular, in the Easterners' reply to Pope Julius in 340, answering his summons to come to Rome.[10]

The Bishop of Rome, thanks to the various titles which made his Church stand out in the whole of Christendom, occupied the first place within the universal episcopate, but this did not confer legal power on his authority. It was the councils which granted canonical status to that primacy. Moreover, insofar as that primacy was originally only one of prestige and moral authority which were merely *confirmed* by its apostolicity, other primacies, independent of "apostolicity" were recognized by the ancient Church: that of Alexandria, of Carthage, and, shortly afterwards, that of Constantinople. On the other hand, apostolicity, to the extent to which it did not have here an exclusive importance, did not entail doctrinal infallibility: it only *added to the Church's authority,* an authority which needed confirming by facts. The Roman Church undoubtedly enjoyed such confirmation during the Church's first six centuries.

THE COUNCIL OF SARDICA

If the sixth canon of Nicaea raises fairly complicated general problems, the decisions of the Council of Sardica appear perfectly clear in their text and in their historical framework. They were occasioned by the deposition of three bishops by the Easterners—Athanasius of Alexandria, Marcellus of Ancyra, and Asclepas of Gaza—and the refusal of the East to accept the revision of their sentence in spite of Pope Julius' express demands which invoked "customs" as instituting the Roman pontiff's competence in this matter. "You should have written to us all, so that justice should have been rendered by all. Do you not know the custom is to write to us first and that justice should be rendered afterwards."[11]

The custom appealed to by Pope Julius, which was far from general (it was in no way applied, for example, in the case of Paul of Samosata who was condemned without appeal by the Council of Antioch), reserves any judgment on an important episcopal see to the whole episcopal body which, in turn, must be warned by letters of the sentence before it accepts or rejects it. The Bishop of Rome, because of his primacy, must be warned first, and he must initiate the verdict of the whole episcopate. The Council of Sardica gave a legal form to that custom, at the same time tempering it somewhat.

Canon 3: If perchance sentence be given against a bishop in any matter and he supposes his case can be not unsound but good, in order that the question may be reopened, let us, if it seems good to your charity, honor the memory of Peter the apostle, and let those who gave judgment write to Julius, Bishop of Rome, so that, if necessary, the case may be retried by the bishops of the neighboring provinces and let him appoint arbiters; but, if it cannot be shown that his case is of a sort as to need a new trial, let the judgment once given not be annulled, but stand good as before.

Canon 4. Bishop Gaudentius (of Naissus in Dacia) said: "If it be your pleasure, it ought to be added to this sentence, full of sanctity, which thou hast pronounced, that, when any bishop has been deposed by the judgment of those bishops who have sees in neighboring places and he [the bishop deposed] shall announce that his case is to be examined in the city of Rome, no other bishop shall in any wise be ordained to his see, after the appeal of him who is apparently deposed, unless the case should have been determined in the judgment of the Roman bishop."

Canon 5.[12] Bishop Hosius said: ". . . If (a bishop who has been deposed by his colleagues of the same province) requires that his case be heard yet again and, at his request, it seems good to move the Bishop of Rome to send presbyters *a latere* ("from his entourage"), let it be in the power of that bishop, according as he judges it to be good and decides it to be right, that some be sent to be judges with the bishops and invested with the authority by whom they were sent; and be this also ordained. But if he think that the bishops are sufficient for the examination and decision of the matter, let him do what shall seem good in his most prudent judgment." The bishops answered, "What has been said is approved."

The essential right granted to the Bishop of Rome consisted, then, of the faculty to judge whether or not there were grounds for revising the trial in the deposition of bishops. The pope did not judge in case of appeal; he could annul the rendered judgment if he thought fit to do so; if he decided, he could also send his legates to take part in the judgment of the appeal to be rendered by a tribunal composed of neighboring bishops from the province where the conflict existed. He no longer had the right to annul that second judgment. P. Battifol even supposes that Sardica took away from the pope the right to judge in appeal and that the canons constitute a compromise on that point with the East.[13]

Without going the whole way with P. Battifol's argument, this author believes that he poses a real question, one which was heatedly debated in the seventeenth and eighteenth centuries between Gallicans and Ultramontanes: Does the Council of Sardica merely ratify an existing situation, or does it introduce a new principle into ecclesiastical law?

The author thinks that this question must be answered in the sense of the generally accepted interpretation of Canon 6 of Nicaea. The Fathers of Sardica did not introduce anything new; they merely transformed a custom, of which Pope Julius wrote to the Easterners, into a canonical rule. The custom already "gave honor to the apostle Peter"; the Fathers wished to confirm this practice by precise rules. They were very conscious of their right to *promulgate* those rules (they promulgated what "pleased" them), yet without innovation in the realm of ecclesiastical structure. This power to promulgate canons belonged only to councils and it was limited by the need to have all decisions "received" by all the Churches.

Our interpretation of the canons of Sardica finds confirmation at the beginning of the fifth century in the case of the priest, Apiarius. This case provides a good illustration of how canonical decisions were applied in the Church, and, in particular, those concerning the rights of the See of Rome.

At that time there were in circulation in the West, and particularly in Rome, Latin collections of the canons of Nicaea which included also the decisions taken at Sardica. For example, we see that Pope Zosimus tried to put into practice the right of annulment granted by Sardica, in his honest conviction that he was acting on the strength of the decisions of the Council of Nicaea. When, in 418, Apiarius, a priest who had been excommunicated by Bishop

Urbanus of Sicca in Africa, appealed to Zosimus, the latter decided to annul the judgment and to have the sentence re-examined by the Council of Carthage in the presence of legates to whom he had given full powers to act in his name according to the letter of the canons of Sardica. In 419, the Council of Carthage (presided over by Aurelian and probably in the presence of Augustine, Bishop of Hippo), in letters addressed to Pope Zosimus and then to his successor Boniface, accepted the procedure, but only as a provisional measure until the text of the Nicene canons had been verified. To that effect, the Fathers of the Council intended to ask for the original text of the Nicene canons from Constantinople, Alexandria, and Antioch, and they advised the pope to do the same. In addition, the Council decided to pardon Apiarius.

The reaction on the part of the Africans was significant in many respects. What strikes us, first of all, is the absolute and exclusive authority given to the canons of Nicaea by the bishops assembled in Carthage. They were understandably ignorant of the fact that the great ecumenical council had instituted a right of appeal in favor of Rome, which, in the preceding year (418), they had formally forbidden under pains of excommunication *(cod. can. Eccl. Afr., can.* 125: *"Ad transmarina qui putaverit appellandum, a nullo intra Africam in communionem suscipiatur"* ("Whoever will think fit to appeal overseas will no longer be admitted to communion within the bounds of Africa."). Yet they were ready to change that decision—and they even did change it provisionally—if only it could be proved that Nicaea had decided otherwise.

Soon afterwards the answer of Atticus of Constantinople and of Cyril of Alexandria reached Carthage. It can be guessed that the Sardica canons did not figure among the versions of the canons of Nicaea which they sent to their

African colleagues. Insofar as the Apiarius case had already been dealt with, matters could have been left as they were. However, eight years later, in 420, the same priest managed to get himself condemned yet again by his bishop, managed to appeal to Pope Celestine, and was accepted in communion with the See of Rome. Once again Celestine sent his legate, Faustinus, to Africa, asking the Bishop of Carthage to rehabilitate Apiarius.

The African bishops then sent a synodal letter to the pope in which they explicitly denied the right of appeal to Rome, basing their denial on a precise doctrine.

First of all, they complained about the authoritarian attitude of the legate who pretended to take his stand on the privileges of the Roman Church (*quasi Ecclesiae Romanae asserens privilegia*);[14] they declared that Apiarius had confessed his crimes and that, as a result, there was no question of absolving him; they referred to Canon 5 of Nicaea (this one was authentic) which considered the provincial council as the supreme tribunal for the clerics of the province. They went on to say: the Nicene Fathers "have ruled that any cases must be completed in the very place where they were initiated: *nec unicuique provinciae gratiam sancti Spiritus defuturam* ("for no province shall be deprived of the grace of the Holy Spirit") . . . Who will believe that our God could inspire justice in the inquiries of one man only and refuse it to innumerable bishops gathered in Council?" To that doctrinal argument against the *transmarinum judicium* ("overseas judgment") the Carthage Fathers added the practical difficulty for a far-away judge to pass judgment on the affairs of a province.[15]

During the seventeenth and eighteenth centuries the Gallicans tried to exploit the case of Apiarius against the right of appeal to Rome. And it can obviously be said that this right of appeal did not exist *as a right* in Africa insofar as the Council of Sardica had not been accepted there. However, the Africans were certainly not unaware of an *usus* mentioned by Pope Julius in his letter to the Easterners, and there are plenty of cases where the Roman judgment was solicited in Africa. St. Augustine mentions some in a letter to the same Pope Celestine about the year 423. But this *usus* was a consequence of the *moral authority* of the See of Rome, and not of his legal right: as long as no council gave any *right* to the Bishop of Rome, he did not possess that right *ex sese,* for "no province is deprived of the grace of the Holy Spirit"; the latter is more likely to be working through the intermediary of "innumerable bishops" than through one only.

After mentioning this example of a rejection of the Council of Sardica in the West, it must be pointed out that it was later received in the East, in spite of its "western" character which some like to emphasize. This reception was ratified by the Council *in Trullo* and put into practice particularly during the case of Photius and Ignatius;[16] what the Roman legates were refused in fifth-century Africa, they obtained in Constantinople during the ninth century. Moreover we have already seen that the fathers of Carthage were also ready to accept this right of the pope provided that it proved to be established on a universally accepted conciliary decision.

THE SECOND ECUMENICAL COUNCIL

The main reasons which, according to the author, led the Council of Nicaea to recognize the special privileges of Rome, Alexandria, and Antioch were mentioned earlier. It has been said that, in the East, the chief determining element was the *de facto* authority acquired by the sees of

Alexandria and Antioch which were situated in the two most important cities of the East. In the case of Rome, both facts—that of being the Church founded by Peter and Paul and that of being the world's first city (the two facts being intrinsically linked from the start anyway) —worked in its favor and made its primacy of authority unquestioned in the Christian world. In the eyes of all, it was "the greatest" Church. For the West it was also "the most ancient" Church and the only "apostolic" one; therefore it is evident that the West, from the time of St. Irenaeus, would be more enclined to insist on the last points, without, at the same time, acknowledging that the Roman Church's apostolicity, by itself, gave it absolute rights over the other Churches. The East, on the contrary, would tend to include the Roman primacy with the *de facto* primacies acquired by some Eastern sees. We see in this the elements of a conflict which was gradually to increase after the fourth century: each side tried to impose on the other its own understanding of primacy, although originally those conceptions were not at all mutually exclusive, but complementary.

The Eastern conception of primacy, as expressed at Nicaea, obviously admitted that Churches other than Rome, Alexandria, and Antioch could also eventually acquire *de facto* authority and enjoy equally the *presbeia.* Such was precisely the case of Constantinople. Historians have often remarked on the role—mostly in a negative way—played during the Arian crisis by certain bishops whom chance or circumstances had placed not far from the imperial throne. The Emperor Theodosius—having fixed his residence permanently in ancient Byzantium which his predecessors had endowed with a senate, a *praefectus urbi*, and all the secular privileges which Old Rome alone had enjoyed until then—decided to increase the authority of the bishop of the capital who, *in fact,* already possessed an exceptional importance. Moreover, this perfectly understandable desire followed the general trend since Constantine which made the organization of the Church conform as closely as possible with the administrative structure of the Roman State.

The Council of 381 published its famous Canon 3: "The Bishop of Constantinople must have the privileges of honor *(ta presbeia tes times)* next to the Bishop of Rome, because that city is a new Rome."

The following remarks can be made on this brief text:

1. The canon conferred *no exceptional legal power* to the Bishop of Constantinople, but specified that it meant "privileges of honor." Consequently, the decisions of the Council of 381 must be compared with Canon 7 of Nicaea which, for different reasons, had granted an *akolouthia tes times* ("priority of honor") to the Bishop of Jerusalem, while safeguarding the rights of the metropolitan of Palestine whose see was in Caesarea, the secular capital of the province. The authority and prestige granted by an "ancient tradition" to the Bishop of Jerusalem were thus equally accorded the bishop of the capital.

2. The Roman primacy was recognized, as it had been at Nicaea, as an undeniable fact, and no particular interpretation was given to that primacy. Constantinople's "privileges" were considered solely as consequences—a sort of reflection—of those of Old Rome. The canon's "point" was obviously aimed against Alexandria whose prestige had been increased by the Arian controversy and whose authority was, until then, unique in the East. No canonical measure, apart from Canon 6 of Nicaea, regulated relations between the large Churches. Nicaea, it will be remembered, simply asserted their authority over a whole civil "diocese" without specifying whether the authority

of ancient sees, like Alexandria or Antioch, could be extended to an even broader area. The bishops of those ancient sees acted sometimes outside their dioceses: Euzoios of Antioch, following the death of Athanasius, installed in Alexandria an Arian bishop, Lucius, and more recently the Alexandrians tried to impose Maximus the Cynic as Bishop of Constantinople. Canon 2 of Constantinople excluded such behavior in the future: "The bishop of Alexandria shall deal only with the affairs of Egypt; the bishops of the East, only with the affairs of the East. . . ."

Canon 3, on the contrary, set in opposition to the legal authority of diocesan primates inside of their "dioceses" a moral authority which consequently had *no geographical limits*—that of Constantinople—just as there were no geographical limits to that of Old Rome, considered as the model for the New. As Canon 6 of Nicaea had taken Rome as the model of Alexandria's rights over several secular provinces, so Canon 3 of Constantinople took Rome as the model for the moral authority of the See of the capital, an authority which was to be universally exercised, independently of the Empire's administrative divisions.

3. The publication of this canon can easily be interpreted as a flagrant manifestation of the caesaropapism of the emperors who, by maintaining the Church organization in conformity with the political structure of the Empire, aimed at putting it under their direct influence. It must not be forgotten, however, that this canon constituted, at the same time, a witness to the Roman primacy and that on this very point it openly broke the parallel between ecclesiastical structure and political organization: it did not pretend that the Bishop of the capital was the *first* among the bishops. Besides, in the East he never prevented the exercise of the recognized authority of the Bishop of Rome. Canon 3 of Constantinople did not imply in any

way that the Bishop of the capital occupied, from that time forward, a position parallel (as a few historians have claimed) to that of a prefect of the praetorium. Its only aim was to modify the order of precedence among the Churches as a result of the newly acquired importance of Constantinople in becoming the second city of the Empire, a title that was still claimed by Alexandria at the beginning of the fourth century. We must remember the contemporary sermon of St. Gregory Nazianzen: "the first city after the first of all cities" (*Orat.* XXXVI:2). Canon 3 was, therefore, entirely in conformity with the principle established at Nicaea, at least as far as the Eastern primacies were concerned.

Canon 28 of Chalcedon, on the contrary, gave a new meaning to the text of 381.

THE COUNCIL OF CHALCEDON

The canonical legislation of the Council of Chalcedon tried, for the main part, to push even further the parallel between the administrative institutions of the Roman Empire and the Church's organizations in compliance with the policy of Theodosius. It laid the foundations of the great politico-religious construction of the Byzantine Empire, ruled on the political level by the *Basileus* and, on the religious level, by the pentarchy system—the five great patriarchates being considered as "the five senses" of the Empire.

Along that line of thought, the Fathers of the Council obviously wanted to stress the importance of the Bishop of the capital, no longer because of the importance of his flock or of the authority of his Church, but simply because his see was in the *imperial city*. That is the sense in which the Fathers of Chalcedon interpreted Canon 3 of Constantinople.

It has been mentioned that this canon granted to the Bishop of the new capital "privileges" without geographical limits: those privileges were now transformed by Canons 9 and 17 of Chalcedon into a right of receiving appeals, a right which was given also, within geographical limits, to the "exarchs of the dioceses," the future patriarchs.

Moreover, the famous Canon 28 was being published:

Following in all things the decisions of the holy Fathers and acknowledging the canon which has been just read of the one hundred and fifty bishops beloved-of-God . . . , we also do enact and decree the same things concerning the privileges of the most holy Church of Constantinople which is New Rome. For the Fathers rightly granted privileges to the throne of Old Rome, because it was the royal city. And one hundred and fifty most religious bishops, actuated by the same considerations, gave equal privileges (*isa presbeia*) to the most holy throne of New Rome, justly judging that the city which is honored with the presence of the Emperor and the Senate, and enjoys equal privileges with the old imperial Rome, should, in ecclesiastical matters, also be magnified as she is and rank next after her; so that, in the Pontic, the Asian, and the Thracian dioceses the metropolitans only and such bishops also of the dioceses aforesaid that are among the barbarians, should be ordained by the aforesaid most holy throne of the most holy Church of Constantinople . . .

This canon included two distinct decisions:

1. A confirmation of Canon 3 of Constantinople, the ecumenical character of which was not universally recognized; the Church of Rome, in particular, had not accepted it. That confirmation constituted also an interpretation and a commentary.

2. It granted the Church of Constantinople jurisdiction over several civil dioceses, a privilege it had enjoyed in practice for quite some time, but which was accorded only

the Churches of Rome, Alexandria, and Antioch by Canon 6 of Nicaea. This second point was in conformity with the Eastern and Nicene tradition, according to which the *de facto* authority of some great Churches could develop into a jurisdiction spread over a larger territory than that of ordinary metropolitans.

It will be remembered that all the canons of Chalcedon were adopted at the Council's fifteenth session in the absence of the imperial representatives and of the Roman legates. The latter having been invited to the session, declined the offer and, on the next day, registered an official protest. Pope St. Leo also opposed this canon in a series of letters addressed to the Easterners, and eventually they yielded for a time to the will of the See of Rome. Only the essential outline of the attitude of both parties will be dealt with here.

The main impression given by the *Easterners' attitude* is the apparent contradiction between the argument of Canon 28, on the one hand, and, on the other, the frequent expressions of praise for "the see of Peter" (particularly in the synodal letter addressed by the Fathers of the Council to Leo) and by their recognition of Rome's exceptional authority in doctrinal matters manifested throughout the Council. In the Council's synodal letter the Pope is addressed as "the interpreter of Blessed Peter's voice," as the "head" of which the Council Fathers are the "members," the Lord having entrusted him with "the keeping of the vine." With the Constantinople Fathers they recognize that the apostolic "ray" which shines on the Roman Church has been transmitted by that Church to the Church of New Rome.[18] The same arguments are taken up in the letter of Anatolios of Constantinople addressed to Pope Leo, in which Rome's paternity in relation to Constantinople is explicitly recognized.[19]

In view of this, how can the content and the argument of Canon 28 be explained? In order to understand that question, one must first see the traditional and logical side in the framework of the principles laid down by the Council of Nicaea: a Church's authority was measured by the actual influence it had on others; in most cases, the bishops of important cities exercised preponderent influence, the origin of the rights they were granted by the councils of Nicaea and Constantinople. In this respect, Rome was the model and the precedent; the praises addressed to the pope by the Fathers of Chalcedon had, therefore, a manifestly ambiguous meaning since, in fact, they justified a parallel elevation of Constantinople. And yet there is a point on which Chalcedon obviously *innovated* in relation to preceding councils: the *criterion* of a Church's authority resided no longer simply in the *acquired* influence of that Church, but exclusively in the fact that it was the place of residence of the Emperor or Senate. This was no dogmatic innovation in view of the previous Eastern practice, but a clarification founded on the recognition of a fact: the Bishop of the capital, in the midst of the Byzantine theocracy, inevitably possessed a real and determining influence. The innovation resided in the very precision of the canon: a new *criterion* of Church authority was established and was applied not only to the Eastern sees, but to Old Rome as well. This criterion was obviously not justifiable historically. It was consistent with post-Nicene Eastern practice, but it was dangerous for the independence of the Church. The innovation introduced in this way by the Easterners had a practical consequence; they were obliged to distinguish implicitly between the *moral authority* which Rome possessed traditionally and the *jurisdictional power* which had been conferred on it since it was the Church of the capital. This distinction was, in fact, the only means of explaining the apparent contradiction between the explicit declarations on the Roman primacy and the canonical decisions of Chalcedon. In studying Canon 6 of Nicaea, we have seen that the indisputable character of the Roman primacy was due to the fact that Rome was, at the same time, the Empire's first city and the Church of Peter and Paul. It was in virtue of its *double claim* to authority that the councils recognized its rights. But the Council of Chalcedon kept only the first motive, while interpreting it in the Byzantine way ("imperial city," and not simply "the greatest city"), although it was ready to recognize Rome's moral authority in virtue of its apostolicity and traditional prestige.

In spite of its "Byzantine innovation," Chalcedon remained in accord with the councils which preceded it on a precise and negative point: although the apostolicity of the Church of Rome did grant it an exceptional authority, it did not confer on it *rights* over the other Churches. Its innovation consisted essentially in interpreting, in a precise sense, Canon 6 of Nicaea on the primacies. This sense *was not excluded* either by the letter of that canon or by its spirit (for it was natural in a medieval State for the bishop of the imperial residence to possess a special authority), but neither was it in conformity with history or without danger for the Church.

The reaction of St. Leo is preserved for us in a series of letters addressed by him to Emperor Marcian, Empress Pulcheria, and Anatolios of Constantinople. Leo bases his opposition to Canon 28 on two arguments:

1. A different interpretation of Canon 6 of Nicaea: Leo adopts the doctrine of the "Decree of Gelasius" which makes Rome, Alexandria, and Antioch three "Petrine" apostolic sees. It has already been shown that this understanding is even less in conformity with history than the view put forward by the Fathers of Chalcedon.

However, Leo was well aware that his scheme of "Petrine" apostolicity, which he wanted to make the sole criterion of primacy, was not accepted by the whole Christian universe. He preferred not to rest the essence of his argument on this point.[20]

2. The argument which Leo used in all his letters to the East was the literal interpretation of the canons of Nicaea which he declared to be absolutely unchangeable. Above all, he sought to contest the rights of the patriarchs of Constantinople over the three dioceses of Pont, Asia, and Thrace, for, according to his interpretation of Nicaea, only the apostolic sees had the right to an authority superior to that of ordinary metropolitans.

The entire quarrel between Rome and the East about Canon 28 comes down to an exegesis of Canon 6 of Nicaea whose exceptional authority was recognized by both parties. In this quarrel the See of Rome won an initial victory: it obtained not only the temporary annulment of Canon 28, but also the apologies of Anatolios. The "Collection of Canons under Fifty Headings" (composed toward the middle of the sixth century by the Byzantine Patriarch, John Scholasticus) included only 27 canons of Chalcedon.[21]

Whether the pope liked it or not, however, the Bishop of Constantinople did, in fact, exercise, since the end of the fourth century, that power which Canon 28 legally conferred. This power was not disputed in the East; it was not disputed even by the victims of Constantinople, particularly the bishops of Alexandria and Antioch whose authority was considerably reduced in the fifth and sixth centuries. Canon 28 thus reappeared in the "Collection under Fourteen Headings" in the seventh century, and the Council *in Trullo* (692) proclaimed it as definitely accepted.

As we have already remarked, this canon in no way

contradicted the Nicene legislation, unless one accepts the "Petrine" interpretation of the latter. On the contrary, it was in conformity with the logical development of ecclesiastical organisms in the Byzantine period which, since the era of Constantine, had admitted the principle that ecclesiastical administration coincided with the secular structure of the Empire. However, this development held great dangers of which Pope Leo was aware, and the East itself did not wish to push it to its logical conclusion. The Roman primacy in its primitive form remained in force and acted as a useful counterbalance to the arbitrary power of the emperors. The Council *in Trullo* itself, which had ignored Roman opposition—this was always possible in the East where papal authority had no juridical character—proclaimed the official acceptance of the canons of Sardica which recommended appeals to Rome in legal cases. Accordingly, throughout the eighth and ninth centuries the authority of Rome was manifested in a very positive sense in the East. And only the schism which followed deprived the East of an arbiter removed from local political circumstances, the universal primacy being transferred for good to the Bishop of the imperial capital.

CONCLUSION

1. Before Nicaea, certain Churches had possessed a special authority and a more or less large sphere of influence, either because of the number of their faithful (large cities) or because of their efforts in defense of the faith, or because of their apostolic foundation. This last point cannot be considered as the only source of the particular prestige of the Church of Rome, although for various reasons it played a major role. The "authority" of

these Churches did not include in itself legal "power": the distinction between moral *authority* and legal *power* is essential in order to understand the organization of the ancient Church and its development.

2. The councils were the instruments which invested some Churches with juridical or canonical powers, but, even apart from these precise conciliar decisions, these Churches—and, above all, the Church of Rome—continued to exercise a particular doctrinal and moral authority as before Nicaea.

3. The Church had become aware, already before Nicaea and mainly through Cyprian, of the universal role of the episcopate *as a college* in fulfilling the functions of the Twelve. The place of Peter was occupied, according to general agreement, by the Bishop of Rome. The latter had, in fact, many qualifications for fulfilling this charge, notably that of presiding over a very great and very ancient Church and of preserving, by succession, the teaching of Peter and Paul. However, this role of the Bishop of Rome could be equated neither with infallibility nor with juridical power over the other bishops, for nothing of this nature had been granted to him by a council.

4. The Orthodox conception of the Church's organization cannot be understood unless the teaching on the universal episcopate, conceived as a reflection of the college of the apostles, is always confronted with the original conception of *each* local Church as possessing the fullness of catholicity. Both approaches to ecclesiology are valid and their co-existence constitutes the mystery of the Church. The *forma Petri* which, according to Leo, is present in each Church in no way prevents the existence of a unique *cathedra Petri*. But the authority of the latter in no way removes the grace which, according to the

Fathers of Carthage, is fully present in each province. A deficiency, always possible, in the *Cathedra Petri* would be compensated for by that grace.

NOTES

[1] This is the text of that canon: *"Placuit ubique et maxime in eo loco, in quo prima cathedra constituta est episcopatus, ut interrogentur hi qui communicatorias litteras tradunt, an omnia recte habeant suo testimonio comprobata.* ("It is pleasing to the council that everywhere, and especially where the bishop-primate resides, enquiries be made about those who come with commendation letters in order to find out whether all the facts concerning them really coincide with the testimony they present.") *Cf.* P. Batiffol, "La *prima cathedra episcopatus* du concile d'Elvire," in *Journal of Theological Studies* XXIII (1922), p. 263 ff.; XXVI (1925), p. 45 ff.

[2] See the analysis of those problems and of previous works dealing with that question in F. Dvornik, *The Idea of Apostolicity in Byzantium,* Cambridge, Mass., 1958, pp. 6–15.

[3] The canonical system in force in Italy is defined by P. Batiffol in the following way: "The suburbican provinces have no provincial autonomy, they have no councils and no metropolitans: the bishop of Rome takes for them the place of council and metropolitan" (*Le Siège Apostolique,* Paris, 1924, p. 169).

[4] On this subject, see P. Gidulianov: *The Metropolitans during the First Three Centuries of Christianity,* (in Russian), no date, pp. 359–364.

[5] According to E. Schwartz ("Der sechste nicänische Kanon auf der Synode von Chalkedon," in *Sitzungsberichte des Preuss. Ak. der Wiss, Phil. Hist. Kl, N.F.,* 14, 1937, p. 32), the original text of the canon which has been preserved by the ancient Latin versions was directed *against* the pretentions of Antioch and assimilated the rights of its bishop to those of other metropolitans. In any case, the "supra-metropolitan" rights of Antioch were recognized in 381.

[6] Concerning the absence of any doctrine of apostolicity in the Eastern Churches, see F. Dvornik, *op. cit.,* pp. 39–105.

[7] Hefele-Leclercq, *Histoire des Conciles,* I, IIême partie, appendice VI, p. 1152.

[8] This interpretation was as popular in the fifth century; see H.

Herman, "Chalkedon und die Ausgestaltung des Konstantinopolitanischen Primates," in A. Grillmeier-H. Bacht, *Das Konzil von Chalkedon,* II, Wurzburg, 1953, pp. 469–470.

[9] *De Bello Jud.,* III, 3.

[10] Text in Sozomenos, III, 8. Herein the bishops of the East manifest their respect for Rome, which is the house of the apostles, and capital of orthodoxy, but they do not accept the role of subordination to Rome, for "Churches are not measured by the size of cities."

[11] Text in Athanasius (*Apol. contra Arian.,* 35). Most Catholic historians translate *outos enthen* as "and thus from here" (i.e., Rome). However, according to the dictionaries of Liddel-Scott and Bailly, the adverb *enthen* means "from there" (*enthende,* "from here," "hence"), "thence," "thereafter." Pope Julius' text uses the words obviously in the latter sense; *see,* on that subject, Brightman, *Journal of Theological Studies,* Jan., 1928, p. 159.

[12] Canon 7 in the Latin collections. The most recent analysis of the several variants of the *text* of the canons is found in H. Hess, *The Canons of the Council of Sardica,* Oxford, 1958.

[13] *La Paix Constantinienne et le Catholicisme,* Paris, 1914, p. 447.

[14] Thus they do not deny the privileges (the *presbeia* of Nicaea); neither do they give them the sense of a legal power.

[15] Letter *Optaremus,* Mansi, *Collectio Conciliorum,* IV, col. 515–516.

[16] The works of F. Dvornik gave good proof of it concerning the Council of 861.

[17] *Orat.* XXXVI, 2.

[18] PL, LIV, col. 951 ff.

[19] PL, LIV, col. 984 A.

[20] Several recent Catholic historians show, on this point, the greatest objectivity in acknowledging Leo's restraint (M. Jugie, *Le Schisme Byzantin,* Paris, 1941, pp. 16–19; A. Wuyts, "Le 28ême canon de Chalcédoine et le fondement du primat romain," in *Or. Chr. Per.,* 1951, III–IV, pp. 265–282; E. Herman, *op. cit.*). This leads them to say that Leo "did not see in the text of the twenty-eight canon the denial of the divinely established Roman primacy" (M. Jugie, *op. cit.,* p. 17), or else that such a denial is really not implied in the text (E. Herman, *op. cit.,* pp. 470–472). It is interesting to notice that the second point of view is expressed by the encyclical *Sempiternus Rex* of Pius XII (". . . *ibidem nihil contra*

divinum iurisdictionis primatum, qui quidem pro explorato habebatur, actum esset . . . ," quoted by E. Herman, *op. cit.*, p. 467, n. 18). Leo's attitude seems clear to the author: conscious of his Petrine *authority,* he does not want to seek for the origin of his *power* of jurisdiction in anything but the conciliary decisions. Hence his insistence on Nicene canons.

[21] V. N. Beneshevich, *Sinagoga v 50 titulov i drugie iuridicheskie sborniki Ioanna Skholastika,* St. Petersburg, 1914, p. 218.

4

*Byzantium and Rome: The Union Attempts**

During the six centuries which separated the patriarchates of Photius (858–867, 877–886) and Gennadios Scholarios (1453–1456), Byzantium and Rome never ceased to consider one another as parts of a single Christendom between which communion could be restored with relative ease. The schism was accepted as established fact, but not as a permanent situation. During each century several attempts were made to end it. This chapter is not intended to be a history of those attempts, but a survey, based on objective facts, of the main reasons for the failure of these efforts. The lapse of time which separates us from the Middle Ages makes it possible today for us

*Originally published in French in *Cahiers de La Pierre-qui-vire,* 1961, pp. 324–334.

to appreciate the scale of the changes which have taken place in the general conditions in which our Churches live. Frankly, many false problems can be dropped nowadays. Historical developments, which at first looked like overwhelming obstacles, can be reduced to their real proportions. Our main task today consists in isolating the permanent tenets of faith which separate us and in approaching them as such. The preliminary clearing of the ground is the greatest service that can be achieved by historical studies.

The Church's union, during the period with which we are dealing, presupposed the agreement among three *de facto* authorities in the Christian world: the Byzantine emperors, the Eastern Church (represented by its bishops and by the totality of its faithful), and the popes of Rome. Since, in the West, *sacerdotium* had asserted its superiority over *imperium,* the pope had, in fact, become the sole spokesman for Western Christendom.

We shall here try to describe briefly the respective attitudes of the three powers concerned.

THE POPES

In their struggles against the various powers which opposed their authority in the West, the Roman pontiffs, from the eleventh century onwards, gradually created an absolute interpretation of their primacy. Neither as "Patriarchs of the West" nor in virtue of a simple "primacy of honor" could they have managed to suppress during the ninth century the autonomy of the metropolitan bishops, as it existed since Nicaea, to reform the Church, and to triumph over the German Emperors' caesaropapism; rather, they were able to do this in virtue of an ecclesiological doctrine which made the Pope sole head of the Church which, within the medieval Christian outlook, implied also temporal sovereignty over the Christian universe. Because of the schism, the Roman pontiffs had completely lost the habit of placing their authority within the perspective of a "pentarchy of patriarchs" (Rome, Constantinople, Alexandria, Antioch, and Jerusalem) which they had accepted *de facto,* if not *de jure,* at the time of the ecumenical councils. They solved the problems which they faced, beginning with the eleventh century, from a Western perspective and within the framework of purely Western institutional developments. Cardinal Humbert's attitude in Constantinople at the time of the 1054 break is obviously an extreme example of this new situation, but it is nonetheless illustrative of the outlook dominant at that time in Rome: against the Byzantines' attacks on the Latin rite, the Roman legates had no arguments other than even more violent condemnations of the Byzantine customs and to declare that the Greeks have "suppressed" the *Filioque* from the Creed!

Without falling into such extremes, all the later popes did, in fact, seek to integrate the East, purely and simply, into the institutional and liturgical framework of Latin Christendom. These efforts culminated in Innocent III's approval of the election of a Latin Patriarch of Constantinople after the city had been conquered by the Crusaders in 1204. In the mind of the Latins of that time, Roman and Latin Christendom normally coincided with the universal Church. In 1205, Innocent III wrote to Baldwin, Latin Emperor of Constantinople: "Since the Empire has passed from the Greeks to the Latins, it is necessary to transform the priests' rites; Ephraim has come back to Judah and should feed on the azymes of sincerity and truth, having disposed of the old leaven."[1]

Although, following the fall of the Latin Empire, the popes became less exacting on the level of ritual, they remained as intractable as before on the doctrinal level. The Greeks constantly had recourse to the idea of a council of union, and on most occasions the papal answer was that it was sufficient to conform to the decrees of the Roman Church. This was the reply given in 1333 to Barlaam, Andronicus III's ambassador to Benedict XII[2] in Avignon. In 1370, Urban V still rejected the idea of a council at which the doctrines of the Roman Church could be questioned.[3] However, some Roman pontiffs made an exception to the rule and were willing to recognize the *existence* of a Byzantine East. Gregory X (1271–1276), for instance, limited the conditions for union to a simple profession of faith; in this way he obtained the adherence of Michael VIII Paleologos to the Roman faith. Similarly, the popes of the early fifteenth century, weakened by the great schism of the West, allowed the convocation of a council which had on its agenda the *discussion* between Greeks and Latins of the problems which divided them, and not simply the matter of the Greeks' adherence to the Roman faith. This change in papal attitude is illustrated by the fact that Florence (in spite of some discussions on that matter during the fourth and fifth sessions) was officially proclaimed "eighth council" in the East, and it kept that title in the first publication of the *Acts*.[4] The latter carefully avoid mentioning the councils held between 787 and 1438 and considered in the West as ecumenical.

In their judgments—often too summary on the attitude of the medieval papacy—the Orthodox theologians ought to give more attention to the radical opposition which existed between the attitude of Innocent III in 1204 and that of Eugenius IV in 1438–39. In fact, by agreeing to hold a council in Ferrara, the Roman See seems to have shown that it could, in principle, satisfy Orthodox conditions for a council of union as they were expressed in 1868, for instance, by the ecumenical patriarch, Gregory VII, to the delegate of the Holy See who had come to invite him to the First Vatican Council. These conditions can be reduced to the possibility of taking up the doctrinal discussion at the point where East and West had separated.[5] The union resulting from the Council of Florence was finally rejected by the majority of the Greek signatories and by the whole Eastern Church, but it is nonetheless true that the ecclesiological attitude of the popes at that Council was a great improvement over the past and, God willing, a precedent for the future.

THE EMPERORS OF BYZANTIUM

During the period dealt with here, the emperors of Byzantium initiated most negotiations for union which brought Greeks and Latins face to face. Nevertheless, political motivation, in particular the hope that the West would organize a crusade against the Turks, undoubtedly was the main driving power which led the emperors to negotiate. Martin Jugie certainly does not exaggerate when he writes: "If the pope had only been a spiritual leader and had not had at his disposal a considerable political power, there would not have been, on the part of the Byzantine emperors, any demand for union."[6]

This is primarily true in the case of Michael VIII Paleologos (1258–1282). He had to face a coalition comprising his worst enemy—Charles of Anjou, King of Sicily—the Pope, and the Latin princes of Greece who, on May 27, 1267 in the papal residence at Viterbo, had signed a treaty of alliance which explicitly declared in its preamble:

> The schismatic Michael Paleologos, having usurped the title of emperor, has taken possession of the imperial city of Constantinople. We are prepared, with the help of God, to undertake the pious task of restoring this noble member separated by the schismatics from our common mother, the holy Roman Church.[7]

Confronted with this threat, Michael VIII aimed constantly at separating his political enemies from the Pope. Thanks to the understanding of Gregory X, he succeeded in doing so, but only at the price of a Roman confession of faith which his representatives, and not those of the Church, brought to the Council of Lyons (1274).

After a fruitless attempt to impose forcefully on his subjects religious union with Rome, Michael was eventually excommunicated in 1281 by Martin IV, a French pope who had restored the papal alliance with Charles of Anjou.

The same political interest was a major factor in all other negotiations of union undertaken by the Paleologi emperors. Undoubtedly one of the greatest mistakes of the popes of that time was to rely on those initiatives: the pontiffs believed they could include within their fold the whole Eastern Church simply by obtaining the personal conversion of the emperors. This showed a definite misunderstanding on their part of the true relations between Church and State in Byzantium. In fact, as Michael VIII's example demonstrated, the emperors, especially in the post-iconoclastic period, had no power to impose their opinions on the Church in matters of faith. Admittedly, they did play a determining role in the election of bishops, the convening of councils, and the administrative affairs of the Church; they did all this, however, precisely in virtue of their function as *Orthodox* emperors. A breach of the true faith deprived them, in the eyes of the Christians of the East, of their authority in Church matters. This explains why, in spite of all their efforts to that end, the emperors of Byzantium did not succeed in imposing union on their subjects; they succeeded only in appointing temporarily unionist patriarchs against the will of the faithful, in that way provoking troubles and persecutions.

Among the Byzantine emperors of that period only one appears to have sought union in a more realistic manner, while desiring it just as much as his contemporaries: it was John Cantacuzene who, like Michael VIII, usurped the throne in 1347, only to abandon it in 1354.

Throughout his career, first as Great Domestic of Andronicus III, then as emperor, and finally as a monk, John Cantacuzene endeavored to keep in close contact with the West, either by negotiating union directly or by supporting the Greek translation of Latin theologians, particularly that of St. Thomas.[8] In his instructions to his ambassadors, in his conversations with the papal legates, and in his own writings, John never missed an opportunity to insist that it was useless to promote unity in the way Michael VIII had done: only an ecumenical council, in which all the Eastern and Western Churches were represented, could effect union. A point he made to the legate Paul in 1367 was that the emperor was obeyed only if his words expressed God's truth.[9]

The project of an ecumenical council, presented by Cantacuzene and accepted in 1367 by the legate Paul, was finally rejected by Pope Urban V. It served, however, as a model for the Council of Florence, the very convening of which represented, as it has been said, an appreciable concession on the part of the papacy to the ecclesiological principles in force in the East.

THE EASTERN CHURCH

The Eastern Church itself, represented by the majority of its clergy and faithful, brought about the failure of the formulas of union which had been proposed in Lyons and Florence with the agreement of the Pope and of the Emperor. In order to justify this opposition, the anti-Latin animosity stirred up by the Crusades, the estrangement of both halves of Christendom, the absence of a common theological language, and every sort of prejudice against the Latin rite have been rightly adduced. These elements undoubtedly played a great role. Yet numerous cases of Christian fraternizing, which resulted in intercommunion, must not be overlooked. On the other hand, the Byzantine Church has always had enlightened minds able to distinguish the essential from the secondary. If Michael Cerularius thought it right to attack the Latin rites in themselves (and even then, in fact, he limited his action to his own patriarchate without pretending to reform the whole Western Church), others who remained intractable on such doctrinal questions as the *Filioque* clearly proclaimed the existence within the one Church of various traditions. Photius, for instance, wrote in 861 to Pope Nicholas I that the unity of faith is the only thing that really matters in order to establish brotherly union between the local churches, while differences in discipline, rite or custom—here he quotes such examples as fasting, the marriage of clerics, and liturgical differences—may all be preserved by Churches which are united in the faith.[10]

Patriarch Peter of Antioch held to the same principle

in his famous letter to Cerularius. Therein he recommended no compromise in matters of dogma, but tolerance in such matters as the beards of oriental clergy and the rings of Western bishops.[11] About the same time one finds the same principles asserted by the famous exegete, Archbishop Theophylact of Okhrid: questions of ritual should not divide Christians, and the Latins' only real error is their doctrine of the Holy Spirit.[12] At the time of the Paleologi, polemicists sometimes revived the eleventh-century controversies over ritual, but these questions were never seriously considered as valid reasons for schism.

The official and constant function of the Byzantine Church was essentially to demand the restoration of the unity of faith through a council. During the fourteenth century in particular, no one in Byzantium was any longer opposed to the actual principle of negotiating unity. Gregory Palamas and his disciples, who acquired in the West the false reputation of violent anti-unionists, themselves took part in these negotiations and encouraged them. Cantacuzene, their great protector, took several steps of initiative in that direction. The most spectacular was the important delegation, civil and ecclesiastical, which negotiated the project of a council in Viterbo in 1367 with Urban V.[13] The Palamite Patriarch Philotheos openly upheld the project and had already summoned the whole eastern episcopate to the Council when the Roman refusal brought everything temporarily to a deadlock. The plan was taken up again in the fifteenth century and resulted in the Council of Florence.

Many elements which determined the tragic history of that Council still have to be studied. It seems to the author now indisputable that the successive attitudes of Bessarion of Nicaea and of Marc of Ephesus, the two theological heads of the Greek delegation—the other members being either politicians or second-rate personalities or abstentionists—were determined by the great separation which developed in Byzantium during the fourteenth century between humanists and Palamites over theological method: the former, favoring a form of skeptical agnosticism, transformed theology into simple rational dialectics founded on the traditional authorities; the latter defended a theology of communion—therefore of true knowledge—which was to be found in the authentic tradition of the Greek Fathers.[14]

After their defeat at the Palamite councils of the fourteenth century, the humanists, a small minority of educated people, felt increasingly drawn to Renaissance Italy. In fact, Bessarion, who belonged to their group, was not very representative of the true Byzantine theology of the time. Marc of Ephesus, on the contrary, was its only valid spokesman. He had also accepted the dialogue with the Latins when he sailed for Florence. However, his refusal to append his signature to the final decree proved to be a much more decisive action than all the other signatures put together. It would certainly have been difficult for the Latins to continue a dialogue of deaf people with Mark: the estrangement, so aptly defined by Fr. Congar,[15] deprived both Greeks and Latins of a common language which would have made mutual understanding possible. Yet that was the condition of a genuine union.

One of the most striking elements of that estrangement was the Greeks' failure to recognize the ecclesiological development which had taken place in the West during the Middle Ages. All discussions of union, from Photius to Florence, were centered on the *Filioque* question. As for the Roman primacy, it was not even on the original agenda of the Council of Florence. During the final days of the proceedings, however, it created a sudden and serious difficulty. The formula of agreement, hastily drawn up, proclaimed the Roman conception of primacy: it allowed the Greeks, thanks to an ambiguous clause on the councils and canons, to interpret it in a purely canonical sense.[17] And yet the Byzantine theologians were aware of the real elements of the question. Several among them had dealt with the problem of the succession of Peter in the Church and had opposed to the Roman ecclesiology the principle of equal apostolicity of all the local Churches whose bishops, by their very function, are all equally successors of Peter.[18] The crucial point in Latin-Greek relations was never seriously discussed in Florence. The Greeks may have believed that, by agreeing to discuss in an ecumenical council all the disputed points, the Pope had agreed *de facto* to consider his primacy as purely a primacy of honor. In any case, their error on this point made them ratify the decisions of a council, the only genuine historical consequence of which was to reduce, in the West, conciliar opposition to Roman centralization.[19]

The final rejection of the Council of Florence by the Eastern Church shows clearly the absence, then as nowadays, of a common ecclesiological criterion between the two Churches. Our times witness the beginnings of a real dialogue on this point, the various elements of which can now be dealt with in a better historical perspective and away from the unhealthy atmosphere of political pressures which prevailed at Florence. May we benefit from the lessons of the past.

NOTES

[1] Ep. LV, PL, 215, col. 623 BC.

[2] PG, CLI, col. 1340 BD.

[3] Baronii-Raynaldi, *Annales,* 1370, n. 3.

[4] F. Dvornik, *The Photian Schism, History and Legend,* Cambridge, 1948, pp. 362–366; *cf.* S. Gill, *The Council of Florence,* Cambridge, 1959, pp. 150–51.

[5] I. Karmires, *op. cit.,* Vol. II, Athens, 1953, pp. 927–928.

[6] *Le Schisme Byzantin,* Paris, 1941, p. 249.

[7] See D. S. Geanakoplos, *Emperor Michael Palelogos and the West: A Study in Byzantine-Latin Relations,* Cambridge, 1959, p. 197.

[8] On Cantacuzene's unionist activity see R. J. Leonertz, "Ambassadeurs grecs auprès du pape Clement VI (1348)" in *Orientalia Christiana Periodica* XIX, 1953, pp. 178–196; J. Meyendorff "Projets de concile oecumenique en 1367: un dialogue inédit entre Jean Cantacuzene et le légat Paul," in *Dumbarton Oaks Papers,* XIV, 1960, pp. 149–177.

[9] J. Meyendorff, *ibid.,* p. 174.

[10] Ep. 2, PG, CII, col. 604–608; cf. *infra,* Chapter 5, "Tradition and Traditions."

[11] PG. *CXX,* col. 224–225.

[12] PG. CXXVI, col. 224–225.

[13] See O. Halecki, *Un Empereur de Byzance à Rome,* Warsaw, 1930, pp. 163–65.

[14] See, on that subject, our *Study of Gregory Palamas,* London, 1964.

[15] "Neuf cent ans après," in *L'Eglise et les Eglises,* Etudes et travaux offerts à Dom Lambert Beauduin, Vol. I, Chèvetogne, 1954, pp. 82–83.

[16] J. Gill, *op. cit.,* p. 281–284.

[17] See Denzinger, 28th ed., number 694.

[18] Cf. John Meyendorff, "St. Peter in Byzantine Theology" in *The Primacy of Peter,* London, 1963, pp. 7–29.

[19] J. Gill, *op. cit.,* p. 411.

5

Tradition and Traditions

Our manuals of theology and our catechisms all speak of "holy tradition" as being one of the essential elements of true Christian life in the Church. This is so because, during a history of almost two thousand years, the Church has preserved the integrity of the apostolic message, has condemned heretics and has defined the Orthodox faith in the face of various historical circumstances and doctrinal problems. She is thus the Body of Christ and the temple of the Spirit of Truth. Tradition, therefore, of which the councils of the past were the most authoritative *porte-parole,* should be able to guide us today in the new conciliar age in which we live. The Assembly of Rhodes has initiated in the Orthodox Church a period of preparation for conciliar action, and no one can doubt that we need the guidance of the Church today. It has been noted that the agenda of the future "prosynod," as adopted in Rhodes, is probably the broadest and also the most vague of all conciliar agenda. These qualities undoubtedly reflect the absence, at the present stage of preparation, of a real theological understanding of the task to be done, and this void will have to be filled before the next steps are taken if one is to hope for any successful continuation of the work which has been started by the Ecumenical Patriarchate. However, the all-embracing nature of the Rhodes agenda can also find, perhaps, a more positive explanation: those who prepared and adopted it may have felt that our present age requires from the Orthodox Church not isolated measures, touching a few minor particulars of Christian life, but an overall rethinking of ecclesiastical life as a whole.

It is obvious that, in order to materialize such a rethinking, it is necessary to keep in mind that the Church, being in itself unchangeable and carrying through the centuries the same apostolic doctrine about the Risen Lord, lives in an ever-changing world. She has to deal with different kinds of men. Our ways of thinking, our methods, education and our approach to life—after all the intellectual, social, industrial and technical revolutions which have taken place—are different from those of the ancient Byzantines or the Kievan Russians. The Church must convey to us the same apostolic faith, but she has to use new channels of communication and a new language which can be understood by us without, however, renouncing the eternal truths of Tradition and the Faith. A distinction is, therefore, to be made between Holy Tradition, in its very essence, and various human traditions which may have served the Church in the past, which may even be very useful in the present as a cultural heritage, but which are not *in themselves* a part of Orthodoxy. Thus Hellenism provided the Fathers with a philosophical terminology which helped them to define our doctrinal beliefs; Byzantium left a rich inheritance of law, liturgy and spirituality, as did Russia. And before our own eyes the Church acquires new historical features determined by the cultures of the lands where she proclaims her message. This evolution of the Church, as a concrete visible society, is a necessary and inevitable element of her life in history: "For though I be free from all men, yet have I made myself servant unto all, that I might gain the more. And unto the Jews I became as a Jew, that I might gain the Jews; to them that are under the law, as under the law, that I might gain them that are under the law; to them that are without the law, as without law (being not without law to God, but under the law to Christ), that I might gain them that are without law" (1 Cor. 9: 19–21). So does also the Church of Christ: she embraces human cultures in all their diversity. She becomes Greek, Byzantine, Latin, Russian or American. However, as St. Paul says, she is also "free from all," for in Christ "there is neither Jew, nor Greek, there is neither bond nor free, there is neither male nor female: for ye are all one in Christ Jesus" (Gal. 3:28). To identify her with any particular human or historical cultural type is to deprive her of the freedom of the Spirit. She then ceases to be the Church of God.

It seems to me that the essential task of the theologians who will be preparing the future Ecumenical Council of the Orthodox Church is to discover ways of separating the Absolute and the Relative in our church life. To do so, they have, of course, first to recover a *vision of the Absolute*. Only then will they be able to make necessary selections in the chaotic mass of human traditions and pass judgment upon some of them. Their task will then be living and constructive: it will consist in rediscovering the all-embracing "catholic" nature of the true Church of Christ. The future Council will have to be faithful to this very nature of the Church, if it is to be a council at all. Its principal aim will be precisely to transcend all human limitations and to present to the modern world a witness to the universal and eternal truth.

It is also quite obvious that a recovery of the true sense of Tradition—as distinct from human "traditionalism"—conditions a true Orthodox ecumenical witness and the restoration of Christian unity.

WHAT IS ORTHODOXY?

A Roman Catholic theologian, who is also a specialist in patristic literature and ancient liturgies as well as one of the most outspoken friends of Orthodoxy in the West, recently made the following statement in connection with the usual appeal made by Orthodox theologians for a "return to the Greek Fathers."

> The Orthodox must understand this: it is not the particular confessional character of Orthodoxy which attracts us. From this point of view, it is not attractive for us. What we like in it is the more genuine preservation of many elements of Christian vitality; but there are also many aspects of which we do not always speak and which we like less . . . This dynamism has led us [in the past] to discover first of all in Orthodoxy the Hellenism of the Fathers, . . . but we also like to go beyond that Hellenism and return to purer scriptural sources of our faith. We also like to rediscover in a not yet hellenized Christianity a freshness closer to the Gospel and the prophets than that which came later. But this is no more Orthodoxy, in the sense usually given to this word. We feel uneasy when any Christian culture is taken as an absolute and we like to say with Pope Benedict XV that the Church is neither Latin, nor Greek, nor Slavic, but only universal.[1]

In an even more abrupt form, the same reproach was made to Orthodoxy by another eminent churchman, Dr. Michael Ramsay, Archbishop of Canterbury. Just before accepting the primatial see of Anglicanism and opening, through his visits to Constantinople and Moscow, a new phase of Orthodox-Anglican relations, he confessed with commendable frankness that he was no longer holding certain "illusions" about the Orthodox Church. The principle obstacle that Dr. Ramsay sees to a rapprochement between the Anglican communion and Orthodoxy is the following:

An Anglican can be found saying: Well, there is a substantial body of dogma which we all believe, but there are one or two things about which some of us would say this, and some of us would say that. Contrast with that kind of thought, Orthodoxy. It is a complete and beautiful picture which is all one whole—and if you smudge it at any one point you have really ruined the picture. It is in that divinely-human wholeness that Orthodoxy exists. And thus the way in which you salute the Mother of God is as much a part of the picture as belief in the Incarnation of Our Lord, one person in two natures. By tampering with any part of the picture, a smudge can ruin it, because it is in the one-ness and wholeness that Orthodoxy lies.[2]

Optimistic in his description of the Anglican position (is it at all possible to discover the "body of dogma" which *all* Anglicans believe?), did Archbishop Ramsay correctly understand Orthodoxy? He certainly did not, if he meant that Orthodoxy can be reduced, as Dom Olivier Rousseau also suggests, to a harmonious conservatory of doctrines and usages shaped in Byzantium and which thus cannot be anything more than one of the possible expressions of true catholicity.

I understand perfectly that our Roman and Protestant brethren wish that this may be true. And many Orthodox churchmen and theologians, especially during the first stages of the Ecumenical Movement, gave some credit to precisely that conception of Orthodoxy. In fact, however, such a conception is irreconcilable with the basic claim of Orthodoxy to be the *true* Church. Once identified with one particular culture, it would be reduced to the state of a simple "branch" of Christianity, which could find its final destiny only in the frame of Roman Catholicity or else in a reintegrated pan-christian "oikumene." Neither of these solutions is compatible with the Orthodox notion of the Church.

It remains, however, that Dom Olivier Rousseau and Archbishop Ramsay have both pointed to a true aspect of contemporary Orthodoxy. They rightly saw that an Orthodox conceives his Christianity as an integral whole which finds its expression in doctrinal convictions as well as in liturgical worship and in whatever attitude he may take as a Christian. The psychological root of this attitude lies in the positive sense of responsibility that an Orthodox usually has for the *integrity* of his faith. He is, consciously or unconsciously, aware of the fact that all acts of worship have some doctrinal implications and that true Christianity is all these taken as a whole. At an elementary level, when he is not able to make the necessary distinctions between the essential and the secondary, he prefers to preserve *everything* rather than lose an iota of the divine law. However, this attitude will be different if he rediscovers a living sense of Tradition together with a necessary scale of values and feels himself able to express it in words and actions. The formal and ritualistic conservatism of Eastern Christians undoubtedly helped them preserve their faith during the dark ages of the

Mongolian or Turkish occupations. However, it cannot be identified, as such, with Catholic Orthodoxy. Today it represents a problem which Orthodox theologians have to handle if they want to face seriously not only the modern world and the Ecumenical Movement, but also, inside the Orthodox world itself, a number of reformist movements (of which the "Renovated Church" in Russia [1922–1945] was the ugliest example) and which exist elsewhere in a less outspoken form.

To re-establish this leading role of theology, a role which belonged to it in the patristic age, is the most necessary condition that the Orthodox Church must fulfill before it enters into a new era of conciliar decisions. And the first task of the Orthodox theological revival will be to rediscover, through a true sense of catholicity, the role of the one, holy Tradition of the Church as distinct from the pseudo-absolutes and human traditions condemned by the Lord Himself. If one turns to the past of the Church, it is, in fact, surprising how many traditional authorities he can find to support this rediscovery, especially in documents related to the schism between East and West.

AUTHORITY OF THE PAST

Since apostolic times, Christians have always conceived their unity as a unity in faith, although it was obvious that every local church could express this faith in its own language, liturgical rite and, originally, even in its own baptismal creed. This linguistic and cultural variety did not at all prevent church unity from remaining a very practical reality. In the second century, St. Irenaeus of Lyons could speak of a unique apostolic tradition equally well preserved in Rome, Smyrna and Ephesus. When christological controversies broke the unity of the Eastern Church, the situation began to change. The schism roughly followed existing cultural and linguistic boundaries, and a majority of non-Greek Eastern Christians—Copts, Syrians, Armenians—adopted monophysitic confessions of faith. The Orthodox Chalcedonian churches followed Rome and Constantinople, and their influence was practically restricted to the Greco-Latin world. Finally, this unity was itself broken with the great schism between Ancient and New Rome, again following radical and linguistic lines.

The prestige of these two centers was so great in their respective areas that all non-Roman and non-Constantinopolitan traditions tended to disappear during a long process of evolution lasting from the sixth to the twelfth century. Both sides started to recognize the ethos and practices of their respective metropolis as the only acceptable pattern. In the East, the ancient Egyptian, Syrian and Palestinian liturgies were gradually replaced, in the Orthodox Church, by the Byzantine rite. In the eleventh century Patriarch Michael Cerularius, in his attacks against the Latins, was already firmly convinced that the practices accepted in the "city guarded by God," i.e., Constantinople, constitute the only true Christian tradition: for him there is no longer any distinction between *the* Tradition of the Church and the local practices of the imperial capital.[3] His Latin opponents adopted an even sharper attitude in their famous decree of excommunication against Michael, deposed, on July 16, 1054, on the altar of St. Sophia.[4] The extreme point of the controversy was reached when Pope Innocent III, after the conquest of Constantinople by the Crusaders in 1204, thought for a moment that it was possible to realize an integrally Latin Christian world under his leadership.[5]

Fortunately, the Orthodox Church has always found in its midst a number of eminent witnesses faithful to the ancient catholic tradition. The process of liturgical unification, according to the practice of the Great Church of Constantinople, did not prevent the translation of the Byzantine rite into the language of the various peoples converted to Orthodoxy. In fact, it was the use of the vernacular as the liturgical language that gave the Byzantine missionaries their principal element of success throughout the Middle Ages. It prevented the Greek Church from undergoing a fossilization comparable to that of the Nestorian and Monophysite churches in the Middle East.

On the other hand, the great Byzantine theologians were always conscious of the necessary distinction between "Tradition" and "traditions." In the very midst of the Greco-Latin disputes about rites and practices, several voices were heard restoring the true scale of values and it is good to keep their memory alive.

Patriarch Photius is the first to be mentioned in this respect. Condemned by Pope Nicholas I on the basis of canonical norms unknown in the East, Photius proclaimed the principle of coexistence, in the universal church, of all legitimate local traditions: "Everybody must preserve what was defined by common ecumenical decisions," he writes to Nicholas, "but a particular opinion of a church father or a definition issued by a local council can be followed by some and ignored by others. Thus, some people customarily shave their beards, others reject this practice through [local] conciliar decrees. Thus, as far as we are concerned, we consider it reprehensible to fast on Saturdays, except once a year [on Holy Saturday], while others fast on other Saturdays as well. Thus Tradition avoids disputes by making practice prevail over the rule.

In Rome there are no priests legitimately married, while our tradition permits men, once married, to be elevated to the priesthood . . ." Photius alludes here to the legislation of the Council *in Trullo* (or "Quinisext") which Rome did not receive. He consciously avoids imposing it upon the Westerners, and finally establishes a general principle: "When the faith remains inviolate, the common and catholic decisions are also safe; a sensible man respects the practices and laws of others; he considers that it is neither wrong to observe them nor illegal to violate them."[6] Faith alone, according to Photius, is thus the criterion for judging the practices of the local churches; nothing else can be opposed to their legitimate variety.[7]

Similar to that of Photius was the attitude of Peter, Patriarch of Antioch, and correspondent of Michael Cerularius. He gave Michael the advice to restrict his criticism of the Latins to the doctrinal question of the *Filioque* and to consider the other standing points of litigation as "indifferent."[8] A contemporary, Theophylact, Greek archbishop of Okhrid, in a treatise consecrated to Greco-Latin polemics, also considers the question of the procession of the Holy Spirit as the only serious problem between Constantinople and Rome. Setting aside the liturgical and canonical accusations of Cerularius, he returns to the principle defined by Photius: "Unless one ignores ecclesiastical history, one will not use such arguments; only those practices can threaten church unity which have a dogmatical implication."[9]

In the fourteenth and fifteenth centuries all contacts between Greeks and Latins implicitly presupposed—at least in Byzantine minds—that reunified Christianity would preserve a variety of local traditions. Nicholas Cabasilas, in speaking of the epiclesis, recalls the Latin rite itself as an argument in favor of the Orthodox position.[10]

There is no doubt that for him the Latin liturgical tradition possesses a catholic authenticity.

Quite recently, in 1895, the same attitude was adopted by the Ecumenical Patriarch Anthimos and his synod in a reply to the encyclical *Praeclara gratulationis* of Pope Leo XIII: the union of the churches can be realized through unity of faith, but this unity does not imply a unification of "the order of the holy services, hymns, liturgical vestments and other similar things which, even when they preserve their former variety, do not endanger the essence and unity of faith."[11]

A LIVING TRADITION

These texts are important for the definition of the Orthodox attitude toward other Christians, but they have also a more general significance in their positive affirmation that the one Apostolic Truth can and even must normally be expressed in various ways. Tradition is a *living* reality, which cannot be petrified into the forms of a particular culture since all human forms, or cultures, are by nature mortal. To disengage Holy Tradition from human traditions which tend to monopolize it is the necessary condition of its preservation. The following are three concrete examples of issues of the most *urgent* nature for contemporary Orthodoxy and which are to be handled by the forthcoming Orthodox council.

1) In the first phases of the Ecumenical Movement, the Orthodox witness was often identified simply as that of the "Eastern Christians." Such a witness had some value in itself, but it tended to present Orthodoxy as a beautiful, but exotic tradition, much too foreign to be taken seriously by Westerners. The texts by Dom Olivier Rousseau and Archbishop Ramsay, quoted above, are

sufficient to show that this form of Orthodox witness becomes irrelevant today. It is not Byzantium so such which interests Western Christians, but the true Christian faith, and this is a most important and positive change which must determine our understanding of the Orthodox participation in the Ecumenical Movement. Today it is neither wise nor serious to speak of a simple "cooperation" between churches, of "unity without union," of "coexistence" between separated confessions, simply because the Ecumenical Movement has been taken seriously by its participants: their aim is to realize *one church* according to the will of *God,* and not a human agreement or federation of churches. Since, for the Orthodox, this one church already exists, they must be definite and frank in proclaiming that the "union of all" is to be realized in the Orthodox faith and that, for them, *this* is the fundamental aim of their ecumenical activity. But they must also understand that the true Apostolic faith can and must be *expressed* in various manners and that the future Christian union will require from historical Orthodoxy great humility and readiness to sacrifice all human elements which at present obscure, in the eyes of others, the Truth which the Church claims to possess.

2) We have already noted that the historical link which tied Orthodoxy to a particular cultural setting—roughly the Byzantine world—has practically disappeared today. This change, in fact, came into being much earlier than it is usually recognized. Russia, since the sixteenth century, and the Balkan countries, since their liberation from the Turkish yoke, have gradually, but overwhelmingly, been "westernized" through the adoption of western systems of education and ways of life. This passage from a Byzantine medieval outlook on life—an outlook originally created and always maintained through the

confession of the Christian faith—to modern European culture (which is at best a "post"-Christian phenomenon) constitutes a great challenge to the Church. The process of "westernization" has brought with it all the impact of modern secularism, and only blind and naive conservatives can believe that it can be fought through a simple and forcible return to Byzantine (or Old Russian) ways, art, music, etc. The old traditions of Eastern Christianity can be fruitful for our generation only inasmuch as they express the *living* Tradition of the Church itself. But life always implies change and growth. This challenge of adapting our Orthodox message to the modern world is a problem for our brethren still living in Eastern Europe and facing the most extreme form of modern secularism—totalitarian communism—but it is perhaps even more a challenge and a responsibility for us living in the West and enjoying freedom of research and discussion. In the United States the "americanization" of Orthodoxy is already a fact evident to anyone who is able to compare American church life with that of the old countries. Even those Orthodox Americans who still have some knowledge of the language of their ancestors think and act as Americans, as they were taught in American schools. They are an organic part of American society. Some people, however, seem to think that this is irreconcilable with Orthodoxy. In fact, they may be right if one admits that Orthodoxy is only an "Eastern" religion, limited both geographically and culturally, a frozen conservative body of customs and beliefs, a part of a dead past. But since Orthodoxy is a *living* Tradition, *the* Catholic Tradition of the Church of Christ, their rejection of "americanization" as such is, in fact, a pure heresy, a rejection of the Church's catholicity. The gradual adaptation of our Church to the facts of

American life is a necessary process. It presupposes, however, a theological and spiritual rediscovery of the Church as a living organism. If this rediscovery is not made by our generation, the unavoidable "americanization" will come about anyhow, but Orthodoxy will be lost. If, however, our theologians, educators and pastors help our generation in this rediscovery, we shall witness the birth of a new, great Orthodox Church, heralding a turn in the history of Christianity, the appearance of a real "western Orthodoxy" opening its doors widely to men of all races and all countries, entering with all other Christian bodies into a serious dialogue about the very essence of the one faith. We should be able to expect from the future Orthodox council some guidance in this present but highly crucial, transitional period.

3) The challenge of ecumenism and that of the modern world should finally lead us to become more conscious of a theologically deeper question: the problem of ecclesiastical structures faced by contemporary Orthodoxy. In fact, ecclesiology is at the very heart of contemporary theological developments and it was an essential part of the agenda of the Roman Council. There is no doubt that here an Orthodox witness is the only one able to define the Church independently of medieval juridical systems and the utterances of the Reformation and Counter-Reformation periods. However, one is obliged to acknowledge that the Orthodox Church often lives today in a way which is contrary to its very nature and to the notion of the Church which its theologians are defending at ecumenical gatherings or teaching in its theological schools. Does the Orthodox concept of the local church—a community of faithful united around the person of the bishop in common fidelity to the Apostolic tradition and in sacramental communion (a notion which the Orthodox

Church has preserved in the face of Roman universalism) remain as a guiding principle of our ecclesiastical life? The present internal crisis of the Church of Greece, the canonical chaos in which American Orthodoxy is obliged to live—with several national jurisdictions coexisting side by side in the same place in flagrant violation of all canonical and ecclesiological norms—the centralism which, in some autocephalous churches, transforms bishops into simple local representatives of their patriarch, the multiplication of titular bishoprics which tends to transform episcopacy into a honorary distinction without any spiritual or theological significance, and many other disturbing signs show that the Orthodox concept of the Church is in danger of being submerged by pseudo-norms and pseudo-traditions. Among the latter, nationalism (or "phyletism") is probably the most dangerous poison. Formally condemned as a heresy by the Council of Constantinople in 1872, it continues, in fact, to isolate the autocephalous churches from one another, maintaining the various national groups of the "diaspora" in different "churches," thus making the missionary witness of Orthodoxy extremely difficult.

Discovery and formulation of all these crucial problems of contemporary Orthodoxy must necessarily precede all conciliar definitions as diagnosis must precede the cure. A good diagnosis is, however, impossible without a true revival of *theology* whose task, in the practical concrete life of the historical church, is to guide it in accordance with scriptural and traditional norms. Outside of these norms, the only real meaning of church life, which is to let the Spirit dwell among men and guide them towards the Kingdom, disappears. Already in the second century, St. Irenaeus of Lyons was writing: "Where the Church is, there is the Spirit of God; and where the Spirit of God is, there is the Church and every kind of grace, but the Spirit is truth."[12] The "collection" of this Spirit requires a constant judgment over "the world," a constant purification, a permanent choice which must be made between the "tradition of men" and "that which comes from God."

NOTES

[1] Dom Olivier Rousseau, *L'Orthodoxie occidentale,* in *Irénikon,* XXXI, 1958, pp. 326–327.

[2] *Holiness, Truth and Unity,* in *Sobornost,* Winter-Spring, 1961, p. 1963.

[3] See especially his letter to Peter of Antioch, Migne, *Pat. Gr.,* CXX, 781–796.

[4] P(trologia) L(atina), CXLVII, 1004.

[5] In his letter of that time, the Pope speaks of maintaining the Greek liturgy in Constantinople only as a temporary tolerance (*P.L.* CCXVI, 902, CCXV, 964D-965A); cf. O. Rousseau, *La question des rites entre Grecs et Latins des premiers siècles au concile de Florence,* in *Irénikon,* XXII, 1949, 3e trim., pp. 253–254; M. Jugie, *Le schisme byz.,* Paris, 1941, p. 253.

[6] Ep. 2, *P.G.,* CII, 604D-605D.

[7] In his encyclical of 867, Photius recurred to purely disciplinary or liturgical accusations against the Latins (Saturday fasting, marriage of priests, administration of the chrism by the priests), but he had in view the Latin missionary activity in Bulgaria, where Latin clergy were denying the validity of Greek practices. There is therefore no essential contradiction between his attitude in 861 and 867.

[8] P.G., CXX, 812D-813A.

[9] P.G., CXXVI, 245B.

[10] *Explanation of the Divine Liturgy,* XXX, English transl. by J. M. Hussey and McNulty, London, SPCK, 1960.

[11] I. Karmires, *Ta dogmatika kai symvolika mnemeia tes Orthodoxou Katholikes Ekklesias,* II, Athens, 1953, p. 935.

[12] *Adversus haereses,* III, 24, 1, Engl. transl. in *The Ante-Nicene Fathers,* I, New York, 1925, p. 458.

6

One Bishop in One City

No canonical regulation has ever been affirmed by the Tradition in the Church with more firmness than the rule which forbids the existence of separate ecclesiastical structures in a single place. The strictly territorial character of Church organization seemed practically self-evident to the Fathers of all the councils, and it is implied by all the canons dealing with ecclesiastical order. We shall here try to give a brief analysis of this canonical legislation of the Church and a definition of its theological and spiritual meaning.

THE CANONS

The Orthodox Church has not, as yet, provided her faithful with a complete system of canonical legislation. It is even doubtful whether she will ever do so. The fullness of divine truth and life indeed abides in the Church, and no juridical system will ever be completely adequate to this living and organic reality which true Christians know only by experience. What, then, is the real meaning of our canons? As soon as we are acquainted with their text, we discover that they usually have been issued in relation to specific situations and distortions of ecclesiastical life which occurred in the past. In order to understand them fully, it is necessary to be acquainted with the particular historical circumstances in which they were published. Then it is that the eternal and normative value of the canons becomes manifest. They appear as a kind of medicine applied by councils and Church Fathers to cure specific diseases of the ecclesiastical organism. This cure is a product of the eternal and permanent nature of the Church. It was, and still is, a witness of the unchangeable identity of the Church, its inner organization and structure being established upon the apostolic witness and provided with the constant presence of the Holy Spirit. The canons indicate to us how to apply to the changeable realities of human history this unchangeable and vivifying reality of the redemptive grace of God abiding in the Church. Consciously to disregard the canons of the Church leads finally to corruption of Church life, that is, to ecclesiological heresy.

In order to understand correctly each canon of the Church, we must, therefore, first localize it in its proper historical setting, then define the particular aspect of the eternal nature of the Church to which it corresponds. Regarding the question which now occupies us—the territorial structure of the Church in the Orthodox tradition—no serious question of interpretation arises, and both the formulas and their meaning are absolutely clear.

Several ecumenical councils have issued decisions on

the matter, and the historical situation in which these decisions were made was not really different from ours today. These decisions from the highest authority in the Church are obviously expressions of Holy Tradition, so that we may safely affirm that, by their very consistency, they express the true and permanent nature of the Church.

The First Ecumenical Council, called in 325 in Nicaea by Emperor Constantine, dealt mainly with the doctrinal question of the Arian heresy. It had also to pay attention to the remnants of various struggles which had divided Christians in the time of the persecutions. Among these dissensions was the schism of the Novatians, a sect of puritans that refused forgiveness to those Christians who had betrayed the faith during the persecutions; second marriages also were formally condemned by this sect. After peace was given to the Church by Constantine, many Novatians wished to return to the communion of the Church. Canon 8 of Nicaea defines the mode through which Novatian communities were to be reunited. Since no question arose as to the validity of Novatian ordinations, the episcopal dignity was to be granted to their bishops, but only in places where no parallel orthodox hierarchy already existed. "But wherever there is a Bishop of the Catholic Church," proclaims the Council, "it is obvious that, as the Bishops of the Church will keep the dignity of a bishop, the one called a bishop among the so-called puritans shall have the honor of a Presbyter. . . . There may not be two bishops in the city."[1] It would obviously have been easier to solve this Novatian problem by giving the schismatic bishops some honorary title, or else by transferring them to some empty episcopal see, or by keeping them as heads of their churches, thus establishing two parallel, mutually recognized "jurisdictions" in the same place. But the Council decided otherwise and solemnly proclaimed the principle of territorial unity of the Church.

In a somewhat different historical context, the Second Ecumenical Council (Constantinople, 381) formulated the same principle on the level of provincial ecclesiastical administration. Because the Church of Alexandria at that time had shown the tendency to intervene and perform ordinations in provinces which did not belong to its jurisdiction, especially in Constantinople, the Council ordered in Canon 2 that, "The Bishops are not to go beyond their own dioceses to churches lying outside of their bounds, nor bring confusion on the churches . . . And let not bishops go beyond their dioceses for ordinations or any other ecclesiastical ministrations, unless they be invited. And the aforesaid canon concerning dioceses being observed, it is evident that the synod of every province will administer the affairs of that particular province as was decreed in Nicaea." The Third Ecumenical Council also declared, in relation to the Church of Cyprus: "None of the God-beloved bishops shall assume control of any province which has not heretofore, from the very beginning, been under his own hand or that of his predecessors" (Canon 8). Finally, we find the same principle in Canon 20 of the Quinisext (Sixth Ecumenical) Council: "It shall not be lawful for a bishop to teach publicly in any city which does not belong to him. If any shall have been observed doing this, let him cease from his episcopate."

A single bishop in every local community, a single synod or council in every province—such is the absolute rule established by the Fathers. In the course of centuries the Church had to protect this rule against many attempts to alter it by the establishment of different princi-

ples of ecclesiastical administration. The importanc
the authority of some churches led them to exer
power over an area larger than their own ecclesi
district and to "bring confusion on the churches." We already saw the Second Ecumenical Council dealing with Alexandrian pretentions of this kind. Gathered in Carthage in 419, the bishops of northern Africa, traditionally opposed to the interventions of Rome in their provincial affairs, wrote to Pope Celestine that "all matters should be terminated in the places where they arise" and that the Fathers "did not think that the grace of the Holy Spirit would be wanting to any province." No bishop, patriarch, or pope can put himself above the council of bishops of a given province "unless it be imagined that God can inspire a single individual with justice, and refuse it to an innumerable multitude of bishops assembled in council."[2] The ecclesiastical affairs of a province cannot be solved from far off, "from behind the see," as the African bishops put it, since the only true aim of Christians is to promote and establish the Kingdom of God in every place, not to serve the interests or ambitions of any particular church or individual.

The same territorial principle was applied in 692 by the Council *in Trullo* (Sixth Ecumenical, or Quinisext) to a case very similar to our contemporary situation: the Cypriot immigration into Asia Minor. Wars between the Arabs and Byzantines provoked shifts of population in the border regions, and one of these shifts concerned, in 691, the larger part of the population of Cyprus which was transferred by Emperor Justinian II to the district of the Hellespont, near the sea of Marmara.

Ecclesiastically, the district possessed in Cyzicus its own metropolitan whose election was confirmed by the Patriarch of Constantinople. Strictly speaking, the Cypriot bishops, who followed their flock into exile, should have submitted to this local jurisdiction. However the Archbishop of Cyprus (since the time of the Council of Ephesus, 431) was the head of an autocephalous church. The General Council of 692 decided to preserve his former right in his new jurisdictional area. The only way of doing so, without encroaching on the territorial unity of the Church, was to submit the Metropolitan of Cyzicus to the former archbishop and also to delegate to him the primatial rights of Constantinople over the area of Hellespont. Both actions were taken by the Council (Canon 39): "We decree . . . that new Justinianopolis[3] shall have the rights of Constantinople and whoever is constituted the pious and most religious bishop thereof shall take precedence of all the bishops of the province of the Hellespont and be elected by his own bishops according to ancient custom . . . the existing bishop of the city of Cyzicus being subject to the metropolitan of the aforesaid Justinianopolis . . ."[4]

It is quite obvious, therefore, that the autocephalous status of the Church of Cyprus did not give her any right to establish her own ecclesiastical administration in places which already possessed a local ecclesiastical structure. The Council did not admit the creation of a parallel Cypriot jurisdiction in Hellespont, and so preserved territorial unity. It solved quite radically a question of precedence at the expense of the existing authorities—Constantinople and Cyzicus—but it did not divide the Church. The pattern of ecclesiastical structure remained the same: one Church, one bishop, one community in every single place. The canons of the Church have always protected this simple principle against all attempts to create several separated ecclesiastical administrations in the same place or country, and also against the tendency of some big and important Churches (Rome, Alexandria, Antioch) to deprive the local bishops of their authority and to affirm their own power over the rights of the local synods.

THE NATURE OF THE CHURCH

The aim of the Incarnation of the Son of God and the very purpose of His teaching, death, and resurrection was to establish between God and men a new relation, a new unity: "The glory which thou gavest me I have given them; that they may be one, even as we are one. I in them and thou in me, that they may be made perfect in one; and that the world may know that thou hast sent me" (John 17:22–33). Unity with God supposes also unity among men, a unity which is described here by Christ himself as visible to the world and as a witness concerning his own mission. It is by seeing the unity that Christians have among themselves that the world "knows" and "believes." This unity is not, therefore, only a spiritual and invisible reality, but it appears in the concrete visible life of the world. Without Christ's unity, Christians cannot truly fulfill their call, because the world cannot see in them the new life given in Christ.

This is the reason why, at the very origin of the Church, "all that believed were together and had all things in common" (Acts 2:44). Christians gathered together regularly for the celebration of the Lord's Supper and nothing—not even the Roman persecutions—could prevent them from holding their assemblies, because the very nature of their faith implied that God abided not in each of them individually, but in the entire Church, the Body of Christ. Only by being a member of this Body could the individual also be a member of Christ. Early

Christians considered each church assembly, held in the name of Christ, that is, in unity and love, as witness of Christ's victory over human egoism, selfishness, and sin. A first-century Father, St. Ignatius, Bishop of Antioch, wrote in a letter to the Church of Ephesus: "Be zealous to assemble more frequently to render thanks (*euchari-stein:* "to celebrate the Eucharist") and praise to God. For when you meet together frequently, the powers of Satan are destroyed and danger from him is dissolved in the harmony of your faith."[5]

No other passage of early Christian literature gives a clearer indication of the very mystery of the Christian Church: by the power of the Holy Spirit, scattered and separated human beings are able to become, when they gather, a powerful and victorious transfigured reality: "Where two or three are gathered in my name, there am I in the midst of them" (Matt. 18:20). This real presence of God in the assembly of the Church makes it possible that the various Christian ministries are really Christ's mysteries, and this applies, first of all, to the episcopal function. Every Christian community is manifesting the Body of Christ in its fullness since this Body cannot be divided: "Wherever Jesus Christ is, there is the Catholic Church."[6] The function of the bishop is to fulfill in the assembly the ministry of the Head, to sit where Christ sat among his disciples, to teach what he taught, to be the shepherd and the high-priest. "Let all follow the bishop," St. Ignatius writes, "as Jesus Christ did the Father, and the priests, as you would the Apostles . . . Let that Eucharist be held valid which is offered by the bishop or by one to whom the bishop has committed this charge. Wherever the bishop appears, there let the people be."[7] There is no Church without the bishop, but, the reverse being also true, there is no bishop outside of the Church, since the head needs a body to fulfill its function. In the views of St. Ignatius, which are confirmed by the entire Tradition of the Church, it is in the Eucharist that the divinely instituted episcopal ministry finds its real meaning. However, the Eucharist is the sacrament of our unity with God and of our unity in Christ among ourselves. The bishop stands at the very center of this mystery. His sacramental functions in the Eucharist liturgy are also expressed in his pastoral responsibilities which oblige him to assure, in the practical life of the Church, the unity given sacramentally by God in the Eucharist. His ministry is, therefore, one of reconciliation and unity.

All these aspects of Orthodox ecclesiology constitute the foundation of our canonical legislation concerning Church structure.

It is inadmissible to have two communities and two bishops in a single place, simply because Christ is one, and only one person can fill His place. This point is of a particular importance today in our dialogues with Roman Catholics who have begun to realize that the existence of one "vicar of Christ" for all the churches duplicates (if it does not suppress) the episcopal sacramental ministry of each particular local community. In the Church of Rome there can be neither theological nor practical objection to maintaining in a single place several ecclesiastical jurisdictions, separated by rite, language, or nationality, because the "criterion of their unity" and the center of their ecclesiastical life is always to be found in Rome, outside their own limits. On the contrary, Orthodox ecclesiology, in affirming the catholic fullness of every local church, is bound to manifest catholic unity everywhere on the local level. The presence of Christ in the Church is guaranteed by the very "gathering in His name," in the unity of the true faith, and in conformity with true tradition—and not by an allegiance to some universal center.

What happens, then, when Orthodox Christians living side by side in the same city consider it normal to constitute several "churches"—the Russian, Greek, Serbian, or Syrian—which, of course, maintain their formal unity in faith and spirit, but not in practice? There is no doubt that such a situation is the greatest blow to our witness in the contemporary world and goes against the very nature of the Church of Christ. Any reference to "spiritual unity" or "sacramental intercommunion" is of no relevance in this connection because Christ has established on earth a Church "visibly" one and because the meaning of spiritual communion consists precisely in giving us the strength and responsibility to accomplish "visible unity."

CONCLUSION

The Tradition of the Church being clear on this point, both on the canonical and on the doctrinal level, the only question which may arise is whether strict territorial unity—one Orthodox bishop and one Orthodox Church in every place for all nationalities and groups—is practical and practicable in 1966. I would answer this question in a twofold manner.

First, by historical evidence. Until the early twenties of the present century, when the united Orthodox Church of America (in the Russian jurisdiction) began to disintegrate into an entire constellation of parallel national jurisdictions, it was impossible to find in the entire history of the Church any example of the territorial principle being overlooked. Do we have the right, then, to consider our present situation as normal?

Second: Orthodox canon law admits what is called the principle of "economy." The most competent canonists of our time are unanimous in defining this principle as a conscious relaxation by the ecclesiastical authorities of the letter of the canons in cases when a strict legalistic observance would do more harm than good to the entire body of the Church.[8] Let us, therefore, act slowly and carefully "for the good of the Church." For a relatively long period of time, we must give the greatest attention to the existence in America of various national groups preserving their national identity. This can easily be secured inside a united Church. National organizations and societies will have to be maintained for the next few generations, and it is equally unavoidable that parishes, deaneries, and even dioceses will preserve for some time their national character. However, a single Church structure must unite and coordinate Church life in America. Various concrete needs can be covered by the principle of "ecclesiastical economy," but division cannot remain a permanent norm, and, at the same time, it is to be remembered that the "good of the Church" which may justify temporal separation requires also unity. The final and ultimate challenge to all of us begins when this "good of the Church" *conflicts* with the interests of our respective national groups. There is no doubt that, in this case, any Orthodox Christian, be he bishop, priest or layman, is bound to put the will of God and the Holy Tradition of the Church above the "human traditions" which were condemned by the Lord as soon as they conflicted with the law of grace. With wisdom and care, let us move toward the restoration of Orthodox canonical norms in America.

NOTES

[1] The major canonical texts of the Orthodox Church are readily available in English. The canons of the Ecumenical Councils are published by H. R. Percival, "The Seventh Ecumenical Councils of the Undivided Church, Their Canons and Dogmatic Decrees," in *A Select Library of Nicene and Post-Nicene Fathers,* 2nd series, Vol. XIV, Grand Rapids, Mich., 1956. *Cf.* also a translation of the standard canonical collection of the Greek-speaking churches, the "Pedalion" or "Rudder" compiled in the late eighteenth century by St. Nicodemos of the Holy Mountain, which has been published recently in the United States by the Orthodox Christian Educational Society, Chicago, Ill., 1957.

[2] Percival, *ed. cit.,* p. 510.

[3] Justinianopolis was then the name of Constantia, capital of Cyprus. The Cypriot settlement in Hellespont was called "New Justinianopolis."

[4] Percival, *ed. cit.,* p. 383; see also the commentary on this canon by Bishop Nikodim Milash, *Pravila Pravoslavnoi Tserkvi s tolkovaniiami,* Vol. 1. St. Petersburg, 1911, pp. 524–525, and by St. Nicodemos of the Holy Mountain in the "Rudder," *ed. cit.,* p. 335. The Cypriots later returned to their home island, but their Archbishop still keeps among his honorific titles that of "Bishop of New Justinianopolis."

[5] Ephesians 6:13, translated by G. G. Walsh, *The Fathers of the Church, The Apostolic Fathers,* New York, 1947, p. 92.

[6] Ignatius of Antioch, *Letter to the Smyrneans* 8, *ibid.,* p. 121. This is the earliest example of the adjective "catholic" applied to the Church in Christian literature.

[7] *Letter to the Smyrneans, ibid.* In the time of St. Ignatius, every Christian community (or "parish") was headed by a bishop who normally was the only celebrant of the Eucharist. Later, with the expansion of Christianity, the bishops started to delegate their privileges to priests on a permanent basis. The parish priest is nowadays the normal center of Church life on the parish level, but he cannot fulfill these functions unless he is appointed by the bishop.

[8] H. S. Alivizatos, *Economy from the Orthodox Point of View* (in Greek), Athens, 1949, pp. 31–39; Jerome Kotsonis, *"Problems of Ecclesiastical Economy"* (in Greek), Athens, 1957, pp. 30 ff.

7

*The Significance of the Reformation in the History of Christendom**

Not being a specialist in the history of the Reformation, I would be quite unqualified to give a technical historical evaluation of the big crisis of the sixteenth century in the Western part of Christendom. What I shall try to present is a theological interpretation of Protestantism as it can be viewed today by an Orthodox theologian, starting with its origins in the Western Church itself and continuing with the later evolutions of the Reformed movement. Since the principle of *Ecclesia reformata et semper reformanda* was, and still is, one of the fundamentals of

*Originally published in *The Ecumenical Review,* XVI, 2, 1964, pp. 164–179.

Protestantism, the Reformation cannot be considered as a single event, chronologically limited to the sixteenth century: it is essentially an *open* movement whose *raison d'être* was and is to *remain* open, to be continually attentive to the Word of God, and to reform itself in accordance with the divine will. It would, therefore, be historically and theologically inaccurate to judge the Reformation only on the basis of what Luther or Calvin have said. In order to understand Protestantism fully, it is necessary to investigate what the Western Church, as a whole, was in the sixteenth century, what was the Reformers' essential claim, and what Protestantism, as a whole, later became.

I

In overcoming the Manichean convictions of his youthful years, St. Augustine formulated a philosophical system, inspired mainly by his Platonic readings which conceived God as the Supreme Good, origin of all existing beings. This idea appeared to Augustine as the most adequate expression of the biblical God to whom his conversion had led him. It constituted a strong negative safeguard against Manichean dualism, but, at the same time, it led the father of Western Christianity to the identification of God with a rationally conceivable essence, that of the Supreme Good. Instead of having an ontological existence, as was the case in Manicheism, evil became a simple absence of Good, since Good was identical with the absolute and divine original being.

In developing his system, Augustine was, of course, aware of the biblical idea of a God essentially *transcendent*—an idea which found another expression in the apophatic, or negative, theology of the Fathers; but this transcendence of God was, for him, relative to the deficiency of the creature, especially that of the *fallen* creature. God is invisible, incomprehensible, unknowable, because man does not possess the necessary vision to see him, the necessary intellect to comprehend him, and the necessary knowledge to know him. However, with the help of grace, man is able to develop a natural capability to know God. This capability is, for Augustine, the *sensus mentis*—an intellectual sense—which naturally belongs only to the *soul* and which is able to know the essence of God, once the soul is liberated from its present dependence upon the body. A Platonizing dualism in anthropology thus takes the place, for Augustine, of his original Manichean ontological dualism.

On the other hand, we know that the Augustinian doctrine of original sin (as opposed, first, to the naturalistic optimism of Pelagius and then proposed against Julian of Eclana as a justification of infant baptism) is based upon the concept of the inherited *guilt* for the sin of Adam. *In quo omnes peccaverunt*: this incorrect Latin translation of Romans 5:12 added a juridical character to the Augustinian interpretation of original sin and provided additional argument in favour of a juridical understanding of salvation. The New Testament doctrine of justification, which is to be understood in the context of the Pauline concept of the old *Law*—showing the sin to be a sin, but also fulfilled in Christ, in whom we are justified for the Law—is thus taken out of its proper New Testament context, and included in a more general metaphysical frame, overshadowing all the other concepts with which the Bible describes salvation: sanctification, new life, union with God, participation in the divine nature. The *massa damnata* of the fallen humanity is the object of God's wrath because it is *guilty*. It can be justified by *grace* which alone can first *forgive,* then restore man in the natural capability of his soul to contemplate God's essence. The latter can occur only beyond the grave; in the present life, man can never be anything else than a forgiven sinner.

The doctrine of God as the Supreme Good in his essence and the Augustinian doctrine of original sin remained intact in the developments which Augustinianism incurred during the period of Western Scholasticism. However, Thomas Aquinas radically abandoned Augustine's theology of knowledge. The starting point of Thomism is the Aristotelian affirmation that all human knowledge starts with *sensible* experience. There is no innate *sensus mentis* which would be able to lead the intellect to the Supreme Good. Human knowledge consists in the ability of the mind to make sensible objects intelligible, and this, in turn, can lead to a relative and indirect knowledge of God. Direct knowledge about God comes from Revelation—the Scripture or the Church's Tradition—which is quite independent from, although not contrary to, reason. The activity of the human mind, which is based not on sensible experience but on revealed truths, is called "theology." It is a natural activity of the mind and it follows all the rules of intellectual scientific research. As such, it is liable to error, and, in order to remain in the Truth, it needs the guidance of the God-established *magisterium* of the Church. Direct *vision* of the Essence of God will, however, be accessible to the elect in the future life.

Salvation, in Scholastic Theology, is conceived along Augustinian lines and interpreted in increasingly juridical terms. Anselm's theory of satisfaction, being soon universally accepted, provides an interpretation of Christ's redemptive sacrifice through which we are all justified in the eyes of God. The fruits of this sacrifice are bestowed through grace which first justifies, then creates in us a *state,* or *habitus,* through which our acts, or works, acquire a *meritorious* character. Grace, therefore, both precedes and accompanies the act of our free will. The Church, which disposes in this world of the gifts of grace, is vicariously empowered to bestow a meritorious character to the acts of our free will; hence her sacramental powers and the practice of indulgences. The tendency to interpret salvation along these lines becomes increasingly prevalent in the late nominalistic developments of Scholasticism.

It is quite unnecessary to speak here in detail about the Reformers' reaction to this Scholastic system. With Luther, it was, first of all, the idea of Salvation *sola fide* and *sola gratia* without anything external to the direct power of God's love and to the human faith which receives this grace; without any meritorious "works" which would be unable to add anything to Christ's saving gift; without all those magical acts, often bought for money and allegedly providing automatic but limited and individual graces. To all the "means of salvation," too cheap and human, offered to the Christian by the Medieval Western Church, Luther opposed the absolute powerlessness of fallen man (which was also felt by Augustine) and the power of the *Gospel.* It is precisely to this powerlessness that the Gospel gives an answer. Man cannot save himself; another one saves him. That is why man has to *believe* in this Other One.

Thus Luther's main intention was to go back to the New Testament, to revive the sense of the God of the Bible, the living God, the Creator and the Sovereign. He recovers the primitive concept of salvation, as a *drama,* a *battle* between God and the evil powers of death and sin which have usurped God's sovereignty over the world. As Aulèn has shown in *Christus Victor,* Lutheran theology was indeed a re-establishment of the basic biblical and patristic elements in this drama. His concern for the Catholic tradition of the Church was obvious, and the Augsburg Confession itself claims to be nothing else than a re-establishment of the ancient apostolic faith liberated from all human philosophical systems. Lutheranism also recovers the sense of mystery of God, revealed *yet* unknown (*revelatus et absconditus*). It is historically probable that Luther was directly inspired by the Rhenish mystics of the fourteenth century, Eckhardt and Tauler, but it is even more significant that he frequently refers also to Chrysostom's treatise *On the Incomprehensibility of God.* And this preoccupation and feeling of the Mystery of God did not disappear when the "prophetic" Reformation of Luther took, with Calvin, the aspect of a strict system. The whole *religion* of Calvin resides precisely in a mystical contemplation of this mystery: *Soli deo gloria.* The negations of the Reformers are all directed against ideas and institutions which seem to deprive God of the worship and the glory due to him alone. When Scholasticism presented the traditions and dogmas of the Church as rational developments of revealed statements sanctioned by the *Magisterium,* the Reformers rejected these dogmas and these traditions precisely as human and rational and, therefore, never to be identified with the Word of God. The gulf between faith and reason, between God and fallen human nature, which was inherited from Augustine, maintained in Thomism, and even widened in the Nominalist Scholasticism of Occam, remained as the common denominator of Western Christianity before and after the Reformation. Rome maintained, however, that God remains present in the created world *vicariously,* through the *authority* of the Church which he himself created for this purpose, through *created grace*—the created *habitus* of Thomism—which grants to the actions of human free will a meritorious character and, therefore, renders human sainthood possible. The Reformers rejected all this realm of created grace altogether as an idolatrous corruption of Christianity: God is God, and man is a sinner. In order to justify man, God does not need man's cooperation; man cannot have any "merit" in the face of God. God speaks, man listens; God forgives, man receives forgiveness through faith. God saves whom he wants to save and condemns those who are predestinated for damnation. And we have seen that the foundations of this lucid Calvinistic logic were already in Augustine.

The later developments of Reformed Christendom are related to these original presuppositions. Scripture, as Word of God, was opposed, from the beginnings of the Reformation, to the words of man. However, the nineteenth century witnessed the development of biblical criticism: Protestant scholars discovered and Protestant theologians realized that the Bible was very much a *human* document. In fact, the nucleus of this problem was already in Luther's critical attitude toward the "straw epistle" of James. In any case, modern biblical criticism brought about a real revolution in a large part of Protestantism. The Word of God is no more in the letter of the Bible, but only in the nucleus of an original "kerygma" which is being defined in various ways and precludes any divine intervention in the normal, natural stage of created beings. Thus, one comes to a kind of thoroughly demythologized deism, extremely remote from the main intuition of the Reformers which was to make a *living* God freely and immediately present to man.

Of course, several phenomena in the history of Protestantism do not exactly fit in this broad picture. I have in mind, for example, the eighteenth-century German pietism, or the Wesleyan fresh approach to the New Testament. But, generally speaking, these movements retained their freshness—and, I would say, their ecumenical significance—only as long as they were not conceptualized and made part of the main stream of Protestant theology. Once integrated into that stream, their influence was *ipso facto* restricted to the realm of "piety," or "emotionalism."

II

In the East the relations of God and man are conceived by the Greek Fathers differently from the line of thought which started with Augustine.

On the one hand, the distinction between the Creator and the creature is maintained, with full strength, especially since Athanasius: divine essence and human nature can *never* mix, or be confounded, or be participated by each other. God is *absolutely* transcendent in this essence, which can never be known, or seen, even in the life to come. The divine transcendence is not due, as in Augustine, to the limitations of our fallen state or to the imperfections of our bodily existence, while disappearing when our soul will be liberated from material bonds: God, in his very Being, is *above* creature; he is always free in his relation with the created world, and nothing created can either possess him or see him. The whole negative, or apophatic, theology of the Fathers expresses precisely this and reflects the fundamental biblical view of the transcendent God.

However, the existence of man, as a creature of God,

is not viewed as a *closed* existence: man has been created in order to share in the life of God, in order to be *with* God. The Genesis story of the establishment of man as king and ruler of the universe speaks precisely of that: God does not create on earth a viceroy, or a vicar, but a being who shares in *his* own properties, who rules not "in the *name* of God," but *in God,* and who, first of all, shares in a quality which belongs properly to God alone: immortality. In other words, what makes man to be a man, and not a beast, is his faculty, originally established by God, to share in God's immortality, in God's power over creatures, and even in God's creative power. One can immediately see here that the problem of grace and nature are conceived quite differently from the Augustinian tradition: grace is not a created gift, given as a *donum superadditum* to an otherwise perfect and immortal being. It is the divine life itself given to man who has been *created in order to* receive it and to share in it and who, if he is deprived of grace, ceases to be consistent with *his own* nature. Man, therefore, is conceived dynamically not only in what he is—a creature—but also in what he is called to be, a "participant in divine nature" (2 Peter 1:4).

And, of course, God is not identified with the static idea of the Supreme Good. Absolutely transcendent in his essence, he is an Acting, Living God. He is not limited by any of the human concepts which can be applied to him. One cannot say only that he *is* the Good: he is, but he is also above all the good that a created mind can conceive. He is both transcendent *and* immanent, because he *wants* to communicate himself to the creature and he wants the creature to share in his own faculties. In fact, the Reformers were quite close to that idea in their idea of *Deus revelatus qua absconditus,* but the whole intellectual tradition to which they belonged prevented them from drawing further conclusions. In the East, especially since the fourth century, it was common teaching that in God essence is to be distinguished from "acts" or "energies," that the transcendence of God is not a prison in which he is secluded, that he is not only free to reveal himself and to communicate his life, but that he created man precisely in order to have him share in his divine immortality and joy.

The fall of man consisted in man's preference to compete with God, to be his equal instead of participating in his gifts. As a result, he abandoned his own destiny, the proper aim of his nature, and became enslaved to the power of death because he did not possess immortality as a property of his own. There is no question, in patristic theology, of an inherited guilt transmitted to the human race through the sin of Adam. What is inherited by the entire human nature is slavery to death and corruption. Luther was recuperating the classical patristic idea (which is taken over, every Sunday, by the Byzantine liturgical texts) that the drama of the fall and salvation was played not in an abstract, juridical, utilitarian manner between God's justice and man's transgressions, but that it involved three sides: God, man, and the Devil. Instead of the Augustinian idea of the inherited guilt—only personal sins can produce guilt—the Fathers spoke of a *personal* power of death and corruption, that of the Devil, from which Christ came to liberate man, "trampling down death by death."

In Christ, indeed, man is given justification before God's law. But he is also restored into the fellowship of God and the participation in divine life: the original relationships between God and man are not only reestablished, but, since God himself has become man, one is allowed to say, with Ireneus and Athanasius, that man is becoming God. The "deification" of man, this central point in patristic doctrine of salvation, is, of course, suspected in the West of being a single transposition of neo-Platonic pantheism. But it would be this only if one held to a much more Greek idea of God as a simple essence. In fact, in patristic theology the deification of man preserves the absolute transcendence of God and his absolute freedom: he *gives* us his own life. In receiving it, man does not "possess" God, he does not become God in essence; he participates in that which is given to him and thanks God for his ineffable grace. This grace is not a created *habitus* which would give a meritorious character to human acts; it is God himself who acts in man's own salvation.

Augustine's and Calvin's concern for always affirming the unique sovereignty of God and the sufficiency of his grace is obviously met here. However, their refusal to admit any human meritorious participation in the act of salvation is simply out of place. There is no question of *adding* human acts to the divine act, which otherwise would be insufficient for man's salvation. The whole problem is not a juridical and utilitarian one—what is sufficient, and what is not; it is a question of the original human destiny which is to be *with* God and *in* God.

This original human destiny has been restored in Christ, the New Adam. He was perfectly God in his divine nature and his divine will, and perfectly and authentically man in his human nature and his human will. In his divine hypostasis the gulf created by the fall between God and man has been bridged forever, and in him we have again access to the Father and become participants of the divine nature. What he is by nature, we become by grace.

No Orthodox theologian will consider that all this is only a Chalcedonian or post-Chalcedonian development of Eastern religious thought; he will read these fundamental experiences of the Orthodox sacramental and liturgical life on practically every page of the New Testament. It is necessary to keep this in mind in order to understand the Orthodox reaction before the historical fact of the Reformation.

Already the Russian publicist and theologian, A. S. Khomiakov, has noticed that in the last century the movement of the Reformation stopped at the frontiers of the Orthodox world, even after it had deeply penetrated into countries like Moravia and Poland which were Roman Catholic. This does not mean, of course, that the historical Christian East was free from all internal diseases capable of provoking dramatic schisms. After the fifth century, the Eastern Church was torn apart by the Christological issue, and the schism between the Orthodox Dyophysites (or Chalcedonians) and the Monophysite or Nestorian communities of the East has not yet been healed. In later times the Russian Old Believers seceded on ritualistic issues, and even today the Eastern Church is being torn apart by similar movements, such as the Greek Old-Calendarists. Mystical sects were always numerous in Russia, but they were never able to attract important masses of the Orthodox population of the country. In the nineteenth and twentieth centuries more or less important bodies of Protestants, mainly Presbyterian or Baptist, appeared both in Russia and in the Middle East. But, whatever can be said of their spiritual vitality—and there is no doubt that there is a lot of vitality in the modern Russian Baptist movement—it cannot be denied that these groups are a pure importation from the West and not a product of the local religious tradition. To see this, it is sufficient to consult their devotional liturgical books. And whatever their future may be, it will be related to the general disappearance today of the cultural and historical barriers between East and West. This disappearance does have in itself a great ecumenical importance, as we shall try to show a little later, but does not necessarily solve the theological problem which divides East and West as spiritual entities.

The historical impermeability of the Orthodox world to the great movement of the Reformation simply illustrates the fact that the theological formulation of Protestantism —at least when it is seen in the light of Eastern Patristic tradition—is fundamentally dependent upon Western Augustinian problematics. However, when one considers some of the essential religious intuitions of the Reformers, one is struck by their convergence with the most important elements of the Patristic synthesis. I am thinking now, in particular, of the idea that saving grace can never, under any circumstances, be considered as *created.* This was, in fact, the main intuition of both Luther and Calvin when they rejected created, meritorious *media* between God and man and also the created institutions which were supposed to "administer" or "dispense" God's grace. There is undoubtedly a fundamental encounter between them and Orthodoxy, where neither the idea of created grace nor that of a human "merit" for man's salvation can find any place. This encounter is simply based on a common understanding of the Gospel of Christ liberated from all philosophical re-interpretations.

Why then, if they are so clearly united on the *Soli Deo Gloria,* do Orthodoxy and Protestantism so widely diverge on such issues as sacramental theology, veneration of the Virgin Mary and the saints, and ecclesiology? It seems to me that an Orthodox theologian is not able to pass a judgment on the matter without considering the Western Augustinian tradition taken *as a whole*. It is from this tradition that there comes the idea that God, being identical with his essence, cannot be *participated* otherwise than in his essence. Since participation in the essence of God—being admitted in the *visio beatifica* of the Scholastics—is irreconcilable with the transcendentalism of the Reformed theology, it is clear that no real *participation* in God is possible. But it is only such a participation which justifies, in Orthodoxy, both veneration of saints and sacramental realism. On the other hand, the Patristic view of *man* as being *created in order to share in God's life,* in order to be *active* in accordance with his own destiny as determined by God, excludes the purely passive role of man in his own salvation. Christ had two natures and two wills, but the Actor was *one,* acting in a divine-human *synergy*. In Christ, our will is active, but in a redeemed, new manner; it does not only "receive," it acts, but not in order to fulfil a "requirement" which would have been left unfulfilled by God;—our will acts in Christ in order to fulfil in itself the image of the Creator which was obscured by the fall but which has been restored in Jesus—in its former beauty.

There is no doubt that the Reformation was a great movement of liberation from false categories imprisoning the Christian Gospel. But in rejecting the doctrines and the institutions which were considered as created intermediaries of grace, the Reformers—it seems—were unaware of a Christology and an ecclesiology other than the Augustinian and the scholastic. An Orthodox theologian can say, therefore, that they rejected not the Catholic tradition of the Church, but its one-sided and corrupt form. They were undoubtedly looking for this authentic true tradition and, in several instances, were practically on the verge of identifying it in the same terms as does the Orthodox Church. In addition to the several instances that we have already noted, the idea of *Ecclesia reformata et semper reformanda* is obviously a Protestant form of understanding Tradition. The principle of the "Church reformed and always to be reformed" can and must be applied, in Orthodoxy, to those elements which are only human, and they are many in the historical Church. Moreover, that which *God gives to us,* the divine presence of his fulness in us and among us, in the sacraments and in the Truth preserved by the Holy Spirit in the Church, is above and beyond "reformation." It can be either accepted or refused. Orthodox and Protestants can certainly agree on the principle of a permanent reformation of that which is human in the Church; where we differ, as I have tried to show, is in the extent to which the human is being *assumed* by God and deified, on the principle of the intrinsic communion between God and man in the Church.

The historical circumstances of the sixteenth century, which also continued until modern times, prevented any real contact between Reformed Christendom and Orthodoxy. Those historical circumstances should always serve as a reminder to the Orthodox of the fact that the Church must not only *be* Orthodox and Catholic through the gift of God, but also *look like* Catholic and Orthodox in the eyes of others. Would the development of Western Christendom not be quite different if there had been some Orthodox *presence* in the West during such crucial periods as the Conciliar schisms of the fifteenth century, or the big crisis of the sixteenth? But in those days, the tragic estrangement between East and West had already been an established fact for many years. Seen in the light of what happened in the West throughout the Middle Ages and the Renaissance, the Orthodox historian cannot avoid considering the schism between Rome and Constantinople as the fundamental, the basic tragedy in the history of Christianity through which the whole of the Christian West lost its theological and spiritual balance. The Orthodox East was often led to adopt toward the West an attitude of sufficiency, and this is undoubtedly our—very human—sin: for it belongs to the very essence of Catholicity to share in the brother's problems and to help him in resolving them before rushing into anathemas and condemnations. However, it is quite important to remember that, while the West was engaged in a series of dramatic crises—the "big schism," Reformation, Counter-Reformation – Eastern Christendom was concerned with tremendous external catastrophies: the "brotherly" visit of the crusaders in Constantinople in 1204, the Mongol invasion of Russia in the thirteenth century, the Arab conquest of the Middle East and the capture of Constantinople and the Balkan peninsula by the Turks in the fifteenth. All this did not favor theological dialogue and spiritual communication, and thus what the Reformers saw in the East was hardly more than a vestige of the past, whose relevance could only consist in the fact that it was also "non-Roman" Christianity. They showed much good will, however, and were quite ready to listen to the voice of the Eastern Church: this is particularly well shown by the personal approaches of Philip Melanchton to Joasaph II of Constantinople (1555–1565), his letter to the Patriarch, stating that he and the other Reformers accept the teachings of Athanasius, Basil, Gregory, Epiphanius, Theodoret and Ireneus. Later the Augsburg Confession was sent in Greek to Patriarch Jeremiah II, and a famous correspondence took place between the Tübingen theologians and the Ecumenical Patriarch. It shows quite clearly the earnest desire of the Reformers to be in communion with the whole universal Church, of which they considered the Eastern Church to be a part, but it also manifests the absence, in those days, of a real common language. Jeremiah II obviously considered the Protestants as being an internal schism in the West and ignored the substance of the issues which brought them out of the Roman fold. This is shown in the fact that he devotes pages in all three of his letters to the question of the *Filioque* which he considers as *the* Western heresy *par excellence,* while giving his approval to the Reformers' doctrine of original sin. Of course, the *Filioque* problem does exist and manifests a doctrine of God which is probably at the root of the main theological issues between East and West; but Jeremiah in the sixteenth century was quite unable to build a coordinated view of the problem. His correspondence with the Tübingen theologians simply showed to him that the Reformation was *not* a return to Orthodoxy, and he stopped the dialogue for which he was not prepared.

The seventeenth and the eighteenth centuries were probably the most tragic periods in the history of Orthodox theology. Both in the Middle West and in Russia it underwent what Father Florovsky once called a "Western captivity." While Patristic spirituality and theology were preserved in the monasteries, in the liturgical books and in popular piety, they were practically forgotten by the few educated people whose schooling was necessarily either Roman Catholic or Protestant. The instinctive reaction of the Orthodox Church against the activities of Western missionaries thus took the unavoidable form of using Protestant arguments against Romans and Roman arguments against Protestants. Both the Protestantizing and the Romanizing parties also fought each other inside the church, while ambassadors of the Roman Catholic powers (France, Austria) and of the Reformed Western states (Holland, Britain) actively intervened in enthroning and dethroning Ecumenical Patriarchs, using money and political influence at the Sultan's court. Their interest in the Eastern Church was mainly connected with their struggle against each other, each side wishing to have the Orthodox in its own fold. Thus Orthodoxy got involved in the Western disputes not in order to solve them, but in order to be *used* as additional arguments. I am mentioning all these tragic events here simply because they have influenced a historic relation between Protestants and Orthodox until today, both on a theological and on a psychological level, by giving to each side a certain picture of the other and by establishing certain habits and attitudes which are not easy to modify.

It is in this setting that the case of Cyril Loukaris is to be understood. This interesting man, one of the most educated Greeks of his time, published in 1621 a confession of faith entirely formulated in Calvinistic terms. This case is important for us because it provoked the first historical confessional reaction of Orthodoxy to the Reformation. A whole turmoil took place throughout the Orthodox Church. Loukaris' confession was condemned by a series of Councils (Constantinople, Kiev, Jassy) where, of course, the latinizing tendency prevailed. The so-called "Confession of Dositheos," confirmed by a council in Bethlehem in 1675, is the most important, and also, fortunately, the less Latin manifestation of this reaction, where the "errors of Luther and Calvin" were unmistakenly condemned.

So an encounter took place, but how much of a dialogue? How much of a real understanding of the issues involved? Neither the historical circumstances nor the theological climate permitted then a mutual understanding.

At this point, I draw some general conclusions.

1. Viewing the history of Christendom from the point

of view of doctrinal development, an Orthodox theologian necessarily considers the estrangement of East and West since the early Middle Ages as the deepest and most fundamental root of later schisms. This does not mean that all Christian theology should have normally consisted in simply repeating the theology of the Greek Fathers. The question here is not in asking for a mechanical fossilization of *one* particular historical period of tradition; it is a question of *consensus* and *continuity*. An Orthodox believes that there is essential *unity* between the Biblical view of God and man and the Greek Patristic synthesis, and this is why for him the Fathers are "The Fathers." Each father may have had his own one-sided views of the Mystery of Christ, and he must then be corrected by the *consensus*. St. Augustine himself is at the origin of later Western developments only because he has been isolated from the entire tradition of the Church and considered as the unique source of theological knowledge. Thus a new synthesis and a new *consensus* took place. The Orthodox reject this new synthesis not for the sake of its novelty—new theologies, new formulations of doctrine are not only unavoidable, but quite necessary, if the Church is truly Catholic and wants to send its message to all peoples and all cultures—but because it is incompatible with the understanding of the Gospel of Christ as expressed in the Bible and the Fathers. However, the Reformation was indeed an attempt to liberate Western Christianity from the scholastic frame of thought and to draw it back to the Bible and to primitive Christianity. We have tried to show where this attempt seems to us to be incomplete. The historical total absence of Orthodoxy in the big Western drama, the lack of concern for the Western developments will certainly be, on the Last Day, one of the heaviest burdens we shall have to bear facing the Lord's Judgment Seat, although some extenuating circumstances will be found for us in the historical catastrophies in which the Christian East was involved.

2. The Reformation, as a fact in the history of Christendom, cannot be evaluated on the basis of what the Reformers had written or said. When one considers the issue superficially, it seems almost impossible to identify the various aspects of modern Protestantism as belonging to the same tradition. However, this is only a superficial impression. In both Barth and Bultmann there is the common intuition that the Word of God and the word of man remain *extrinsic* to each other. The development followed by Barth in his later works and leading to a new discovery of the Word of God in the created world, to a solidarity between God and man in the *natural* order—this idea was always strong in the West, both in Thomism and in modern liberalism, and was also stressed by Russian sophiologists—is still quite different from the notion of a *free* mutual participation of God and man *in the Church* through the Word's historic incarnation. Thus, whether one holds an optimistic anthropology, so widespread in American Protestantism, or the pessimistic Calvinistic remembrance of sin still holding humanity, whether one considers God as the Forgiver or simply as a nice heavenly Father who has nothing to forgive, it remains that the life of the Christian in the Church does not *participate* in God's life. Hence, of course, in both the "neo-Orthodox" and in the "liberal" camp of Protestantism, many hold as indifferent for the essential Christian *kerygma* whether Christ was God or not, whether his Resurrection was or was not a historical fact. And then one is bound to ask oneself what is left of the Biblical and Patristic synthesis and of Christianity in general—this Christianity that every Orthodox *does experience* on the practical and "naive"

level of Protestant worship and life which are still mainly in the line of the ancient tradition. For the Orthodox, the essence of the Gospel resides precisely in fact that God *does* speak through the human lips of the historical God-man Jesus who rose from the dead; he speaks in the Bible, in the tradition, in the sacramental structure of the Church, in the personalities of saints. God *has given us* all this without prejudice to his essential transcendence.

3. My third and final conclusion concerns the Ecumenical Movement. Orthodox ecclesiology is based upon the unity of local churches recognizing in each other the same faith, the same sacramental divine presence, and witnessing to this unity through common action and communion of spirit and life. Schism occurs when this mutual recognition disappears. This happened between the East and the West in the early Middle Ages. The Reformation produced in the West a new situation, but the first superficial attempts made by the Orthodox to recognize in the Reformed communities the same revealed fulness of Christ's truth and presence failed. The Ecumenical Movement is today the continuation of these efforts of recognition. They represent a necessary and absolute condition for communion in faith and sacraments. They bring mutual knowledge, hence their theological and ecclesiological significance, even if—and this does unfortunately happen—they produce disappointment and frustration. Frustration, pain and suffering are unavoidable whenever there is error and schism until they are cured.

Now, we can ask ourselves how much mutual knowledge and understanding has there been achieved? The least that one can answer is that we are still at the very beginning of the road, if one considers the situation of the two spiritual worlds to which we belong. We have a lot more to do. But on the way it is essential not to get lost in byways. Let us frankly face the issue: Does the present structure of the World Council reflect the real theological and spiritual situation of the Christian world? How much place is given to the dialogue between Orthodoxy and Protestantism as two entities? It is in such a dialogue that the real issue is to be solved, as we have tried to show. It is not clear, anyhow, that the problem of uniting Methodists and Presbyterians with each other is of a quite different nature from that which confronts the relations between Orthodoxy and Protestantism as a whole? In the present institutional and psychological situation of the World Council of Churches, the Orthodox Church looks, however, as if it were an extreme right wing of non-Roman Christianity, a kind of super-high church, exotic, irrelevant in its solemnity.

The Orthodox themselves are, to a very large extent, responsible for this situation. Their way of being represented in the World Council without the necessary theological preparation and personnel, limiting themselves to separate declarations—obviously necessary in themselves but insufficient to replace a real participation and influence in the ecumenical debate—confuses the issues in the eyes of many. There must be a new stage in our relations.

We are living in a time when many of the old issues can now be more easily clarified. The historical estrangement of East and West—linguistic, spiritual, intellectual—is bound to disappear in a world which becomes too small. The "non-theological" elements of our estrangement will soon belong to the past. Orthodoxy today is no more—and will become less and less—an "Eastern" Church, just as Western Christianity ceases to be only "Western." This will help us to forget the relative issues and concentrate on the real ones. Let us see in all this the hand of God.

8

*Vatican II**

EXPECTATIONS

Pope John XXIII's announcement of the Council seemed to most Christians a revolutionary event in itself. Many, inside as well as outside the Roman Church, thought that the decisions of 1870 were irreconcilable with the idea of councils. Since there was already in existence a visible organ of infallibility which, in conformity with the conscience of the Church, could express *ex sese* the verities of the faith, and since, moreover, this organ was invested with immediate jurisdiction over all faithful Catholics and could thus guide them directly and permanently in all the problems of Christian conscience in the modern world—what reason was there for holding a council?

*The first part of this chapter was originally published in *Cross Currents*, December, 1961.

The manner in which the announcement was made, by Pope John himself, on his own initiative and before Vatican officials could make a preliminary study of possible repercussions, accentuated still further the effect of surprise. In fact, it does not seem that John XXIII was posing the problem of whether the holding of a council was reconcilable with Vatican dogma, but that he was simply affirming the fact that the conciliary institution was an integral part of Catholic ecclesiology and that Vatican dogma must be interpreted in terms of this permanent and necessary state of affairs. His various declarations relative to the Council, his desire to accentuate his own function as "Bishop of Rome," a local bishop, "brother" of all the bishops of the world—Pius XII, on the contrary, used to emphasize his "universal episcopate"—and, finally, his desire to pose the problem of Christian unity in a new way, all showed that John XXIII was insisting upon a true return to the sources of Christian tradition.

In the Orthodox world, reactions were numerous and, on the whole, sympathetic. That reservations and criticisms were also heard was only natural after centuries of mutual ignorance and often justified distrust and in the face of actual political circumstances. It remains true, nonetheless, that the Orthodox Church, since the time of the separation, has asked the West to question itself on the medieval developments of its theology and ecclesiology and to judge them in accordance with the most ancient tradition. Certainly Orthodox spokesmen of the last century sometimes even dreamed of a pope's proclaiming *ex cathedra* his own non-infallibility and thus assuring union of the churches. We have obviously not yet reached that point, but it is clear that John XXIII was not content merely to wish for union; rather, he conceived of unity as a problem both external and internal to the Church of

Rome itself. In convoking the Council he was trying to create, within the Roman Church, the conditions under which the union of Christians might become possible. It is in this self-questioning by the Catholic Church that there lies the great hope of unity.

The Roman West and Orthodox hold in common the idea that, in the Incarnation, Christ, by becoming historic man, wished for the existence on earth of a visible community—as visible as His own humanity—to which He promised a Spirit which would guide it in truth. This idea of a Church, one and infallible, was the common heritage of East and West throughout the first millennium of Christian history. What today divides us is, above all, the gigantic ecclesiological development produced in the West since the Gregorian reformation. Even in the seventh century, according to Pope Gregory the Great (d. 604), the idea of a "universal bishop"—the Pope thus interpreted the title of "ecumenical patriarch" which had just been conferred upon the Archbishop of Constantinople—was "a rash pretension which disturbed the peace of the entire Church,"[1] "a blasphemy attributing to a single bishop a dignity which suppressed that of all the rest."[2] Since then, in the West, the title of "universal bishop" has not only become common usage; it has been an article of faith since the First Vatican Council: the jurisdiction of the pope over the entire body of the faithful of the universal Church is a jurisdiction that is "immediate" and "truly episcopal."

An evolution, or, as the theologians say, a "development of dogma" has indisputably occurred, therefore; on its part, the Christian East has not followed. The notion of "doctrinal development" implies that truth, considered as only implicit in the first centuries of the Church, becomes only progressively explicit. Modern Catholic apologists like to collect citations from the Fathers and from councils indicating the widespread understanding, in East and West alike, of Roman infallibility in ancient times. The Orthodox willingly admit that these florilegia indicate the reality of a certain authority for the Roman Church: they speak of a "preeminence of honor," of "prestige," and of "priority" in the common affairs of local churches; they recognize that these ideas would benefit from precise formulation by modern Orthodox theology, and that they constitute an important ecclesiological problem for the Church today.[3] But the Orthodox also affirm an essential fact of the life of the ancient Church: when a question of faith was posed for Christians, its solution was the province of the conscience *of all* the local churches. Conciliary procedure was then resorted to. Once the question was settled—with the active or passive participation of Rome, sometimes without that participation—the discussions very often *continued:* they were terminated either by the disappearance of the heresy, by an authoritative commentary on the definition which satisfied the malcontents, or, finally, by schism. The *criterion* was always *truth itself,* and not a visible organ of infallibility.

This absence of a juridical criterion made a Christian of the first centuries a man both free and responsible. His freedom, moreover, was not a formal freedom of the individual: for a Christian there is no freedom outside truth, outside Christ and the Holy Spirit, outside the Church. But the Church, for the primitive Christian, was, above all, a *communion* and not an external criterion of doctrinal security. The primitive Christian was an active member of a living body; in the life of this body resided the miracle of infallibility and permanence. In the sacramental reality of the Eucharist, fully realized in every local community, communion to the Catholic body of the

Church was accessible to all through baptism, in union with the saints of the past, and in unity with all those who shared the same fidelity in Christ. The men who were invested with the *magisterium*—the bishops—were themselves in the service of this communion; they were its principal ministers but they did not in themselves determine it; they had to accomplish *within* the Church, not above it, their ministry as guardians of the apostolic tradition.

The pre-eminence of the Roman Church of the first centuries, recognized and in part defined by the ancient councils, was itself one of the *instruments* of this communion. When, in the Middle Ages, this pre-eminence became a definitive criterion, the whole ecclesiological perspective was modified. Soon an important part of Western Christianity felt itself deprived of fundamental Christian liberty and was driven into revolt. The Protestant revolt was followed by many others, still more negative ones, all of which opposed the Church in the name of freedom. The Church more and more identified itself with the idea of unconditional and infallible authority. This identification was the more patent as the Roman Church, in the face of the revolts, became more and more rigid: the Church defined, codified, and passed legislation upon the Mystery to try to protect it; at last the definition of infallibility and immediate jurisdiction appeared. Purely human elements, of a social and political kind, played a well-known role in this last definition.

Reformation and Counter-Reformation thus set off a long chain reaction which in large measure defined the history of Western Christianity in the last four centuries.

Had John XXIII mounted the throne of Peter to stop this movement, which has been in process since Gregory VII, and to give it a less desperate direction? The Council was called upon to answer this question, and the union of Christians depended upon the solution it was able to provide.

Modern Catholic "unionism" is connected, in the main, with three modes of thinking which define three methods practiced in approaching the Orthodox.

1. A small group of theologians adheres quite simply to the old polemical method which consists in showing that the adversary is completely inconsistent and can inspire only a charitable pity. The Council has already disavowed this attitude.

2. A second group of theologians and ecumenists affirms, on the contrary, that there are only misunderstandings between Orthodoxy and Rome; no serious doctrinal difference keeps the two great historic churches of the East and the West in opposition. When others attempt to raise questions of dogma, this group even questions their intentions: Why create problems as long as the Orthodox can find, in embryo, in their own Eastern tradition all the doctrine which Rome has explicitly formulated? All that is needed to create unity is for the two parties to change their psychological attitude and abandon their prejudices and misunderstandings. At this point Roman primacy will appear a providential instrument which gives the Church the necessary flexibility to integrate—within itself, naturally—those different rituals and traditions whose very variety and multiplicity constitute the best sign of true catholicity.

3. A third group, while generally sharing the desire for greater openness characteristic of the preceding group, differs from it on one essential point. They admit the enormous doctrinal and institutional problem represented, for the Orthodox, by the Roman Church in its present state; they share this difficulty from inside and wish the

Roman positions to be reformulated, if not modified. This desire stems not from a special "interest in problems of unity"; rather, it is a desire to see the Church of Christ as Christ wanted it to be. This attitude springs from a truly theocentric spirituality common to all, Catholic or non-Catholic, who are concerned with bearing Christian witness in the modern world and do not believe that everything can be solved by ecclesiastical politics. With theologians of this spirit, the Orthodox will not be ashamed to make a self-criticism and recognize the historic deficiencies of his own Church; he will be ready to share in the search for the single truth.

Under the pontificate of Pius XII the Roman attitude was largely determined by the first group and to a certain degree by the second. The really new aspect noted in the conduct of John XXIII was that the Pope himself seemed to belong to the third group. His personal friendships before the pontificate (notably that which allied him to Dom Beauduin Lambert), his experience of Eastern Christian affairs, and the numerous public disavowals he has addressed to polemicists and denigrators constituted the great hope of the Council.

It was obvious from the start that everything would not be resolved. There would be no discussion of *Filioque,* of original sin, or of sacramental theology. There would be discussion, above all, of the Church. In this respect, the success or failure of the Council—on the unionist level—depended upon the content of the additions which could (or could not) be borne by the definitions of 1870 which affirmed: (1) the infallibility *ex cathedra* and *ex sese, non autem ex consensu ecclesiae;* (2) the "immediate" and "truly episcopal" jurisdiction by the pope over all the faithful.

The dogma of infallibility aroused furious polemic

before and after its publication. Pius IX himself, after the Council, partly moderated its effect in his correspondence with the German bishops. Progressive Catholic theologians generally admitted that the redaction of the dogma was unfortunate in the degree to which absolute and, for many, frightening terminology like "infallibility" and *ex sese,* was used in a rather imprecise context. Indeed, these terms can be understood in the most "integralist" sense, though they are susceptible of moderate interpretation as well. Thus the possible distinction between *consensus* and *sensus ecclesiae* is invoked by those who wish to give a "liberal" interpretation to Vatican I. According to them, the Council of 1870, in excluding the *consensus ecclesiae* from the conditions requisite for a definition of infallibility, wished simply to discard the juridical idea of a majority and "democratic" vote. As to the *sensus ecclesiae,* this vital and organic aspect of the Church which has always been identical with itself since apostolic times must keep control over the pope as well as over the other bishops and all Christians, both in his *ex cathedra* statements as in his other acts.[4] An interpretation of the definition of 1870 along this line would certainly open a very large door to subsequent dialogue between Rome and Orthodoxy. Because, finally, for the Orthodox Church, too, the seat of infallibility is not the majority vote; it is, rather, this *sensus ecclesiae* which is fundamentally nothing other than the Holy Spirit dwelling in the Church.

The problem of immediate jurisdiction—a less noted and less discussed aspect of the decisions of 1870—apparently presents difficulties at least as great as those of infallibility.[5] The text assumes in effect that the pope exercises his function as universal pastor directly over all the faithful, and for this does not need the bishops even as intermediaries. A certain tendency in modern Catholic ecclesiology even suggested—before Vatican II—the possibility of a still greater limitation of the role of the episcopate, a functional institution whose immediate utility might eventually disappear. The Holy See, with the aid of the religious orders, would be able to provide for the whole administration of the universal Church. This was obviously not the official interpretation of the dogma of 1870, but a possible development of the decision on "immediate jurisdiction." On the practical level, in any case, "immediate jurisdiction" renders the Catholic Church suspect in all countries where the political philosophy does not correspond to that advanced by the Roman encyclicals.

This seems to have been what limited John F. Kennedy's majority to 100,000 votes in the American Presidential elections of November, 1960. It also permitted Rome to suppress the experiment of the worker-priests in France without the French bishops being able seriously to undertake the defense of this particular aspect of their pastoral concern for the flock which God confided to them.

The problem of the episcopate, which the First Vatican Council did not have time to examine, was, therefore, one of the main issues of Vatican II: a viable definition was to be sought, on the one hand, for the traditional bond between the bishop and his diocese and, on the other, for the relation between the bishops and Rome. The definition which the Catholic Church would give to its own internal structure would, in large measure, determine the perspectives of Christian unity. The Orthodox Church for its part has always confessed the impossibility of a bishop's exercising a power of divine right over another bishop or over the community presided over by another bishop; Orthodox ecclesiology is, in fact, founded upon the essential identity—in a single sacramental reality and a single apostolic succession—of all the local churches.

Clearly, it was not easy for the fathers of the Second

Vatican Council to bring important correctives to bear upon the decisions of 1870. The centralized structure which, under Pius IX, received absolute dogmatic and religious foundation confers—apparently, at least—a formidable efficacy upon the Roman Catholic Church. Can one lightheartedly renounce even a part of that efficacy? And the Orthodox Church, in its contemporary aspect, is far from being able to serve in all things as a very attractive model. However, when it is a matter of the religion of the Gospels, the problem of efficacy can no longer be treated as it is on the human level. The efficacy of the Spirit of God does not obey the laws of wordly success: the existence, in 1966, of millions of Orthodox Christians in Russia proves that the life of the Church does not depend upon political systems or upon ecclesiastical centralizations built up in the Middle Ages. And, finally, is not the problem of our time one of detachment with regard to the philosophical, social, or political doctrines which are collapsing under our eyes? In recognizing this collapse we obviously risk accepting as absolute the new systems which are now taking form; one easily becomes modernist by merging with bad alloys. But it is certainly not an indication of modernism to return to the sources of the Christian tradition in order to find there the absolute and permanent kernel of truth. Such a return is the condition of unity.

RESULTS

It would be obviously impossible to give here, in these few pages, a full analysis of the results of Vatican Council II. On the purely theological level, the Constitution on Revelation is likely to have the most lasting effect since, by discarding the doctrine of the "two sources" of Revelation—one of the battle cries of the Counter-Reformation—it establishes a relation between Scripture and Tradition which, in fact, enhances both in their true and positive meaning: while encouraging the Biblical revival in Catholicism it presents a concept of Tradition toward which, under the impact of Ecumenism, a large section of Protestantism is also moving.

The opening to the world — secular, non-Christian, Marxist—which was called for by the Council received the press headlines and certainly endorses a dimension of the Gospel which had been previously overlooked; it also assumes much of the "secular" concerns of modern Protestant thought (including some of its more questionable elements) and establishes a basis for a common Christian action in social matters. The implications of all these aspects of the Vatican decisions would need a special study which would go beyond the scope of our concern here. We shall limit ourselves, therefore, to remarks on the texts which have the greatest bearing upon relations between Orthodox and Catholics. These are the Constitutions on the Liturgy, on the Church, and on Ecumenism.

It is clear, in the first place, that the real significance of the decrees adopted will be fully revealed only through the manner in which they are put into effect. On the psychological and practical level, however, the results are already visible. The Constitution on the Liturgy is adjusting the Church's practice to the demands of the times and to the recent findings of the Liturgical Movement; the decisions on ecumenism are revolutionizing the attitude of the Roman Catholic world toward other Christians, and are setting the scene for a dialogue which is only at its start and may produce important and perhaps unexpected results; the creation of a married diaconate marks an end to a certain clericalism which has, over the centuries, shaped the image of the Roman Church in the eyes of the world outside. As with all practical reforms, however, these measures are giving rise to new problems. For example, one may ask the question whether the various determinations of the liturgical reform will not be limiting the element of "mystery" in worship and especially in the Eucharist? Will not the use of the vernacular, while making the liturgy accessible to the faithful, tend, over a more or less short space of time, to reinforce the spirit of "national Churches" to the detriment of Roman unity—a spirit whose disadvantages, as well as advantages, Orthodoxy has known for a long time, having accepted the use of national languages in the liturgy from the beginning? On the other hand, do not the interpretations being given to the new diaconate and the functions being attributed to it—preaching, the administration, where necessary, of practically all the sacraments—create basically a kind of new priesthood of a second order? Certainly these were not the original functions of the diaconate: the deacon was not a substitute for the priest, but an assistant of the bishop in the administration of particular aspects of ecclesiastical life, especially those of a social nature.

In short, the rather secondary problem of the diaconate illustrates very well an important spiritual and pschological fact: for the majority of the members of the Council it has not been so much a matter of rediscovering the eternal or theological, ecclesiological, norms of the Church's life, as of adapting an old and familiar ecclesiology, whose existing structures date from the Middle Ages, to the realities and exigencies of the modern world. It was, of course, impossible to expect anything else from Vatican II; from the beginning the Roman Church has been a Church of Tradition, the latter being understood as an organic development stemming from an apostolic embryo and providing through successive stages an ever more complete explanation of Revelation. The Church, therefore, cannot simply jump over the Middle Ages back to primitive Christianity. Anyway, an episcopate formed under Pius X and Pius XII could not have adopted a constitution really revolutionary.

The problem of the ecclesiology contained either explicitly or implicitly in the decisions of the Council must, therefore, be the main subject of our dialogue in the years to come. It is this ecclesiology, erected in the Middle Ages and still present in the background of all the inner developments of the Roman Church, which constitutes the basic doctrinal and spiritual obstacle to union.

We shall examine briefly here two aspects of the decisions of Vatican II: the new attitude toward "ecumenism" and the decisions concerning the episcopate. The relations between Rome and Orthodoxy will be largely determined by these decisions which, in all events, are rightly considered as the most important achievements of Vatican II.

All Roman Catholic ecumenism—and all Orthodox ecumenism for that matter—presupposes the visible existence of the *one* Church from which all other Christian communities are "separated." But, while for Orthodoxy this given unity of the Church is manifested by a community of faith and a unity having Christ and the Holy Spirit as its final criteria, Rome maintains that there is also a given structure of the universal Church, founded on the primacy, infallibility and immediate jurisdiction of the See of Peter which has divine and supernatural origin. Two concepts of ecumenism stem from this fundamental difference in ecclesiology and are reflected in the practical attitude and especially in the mentality of the two Churches. While admitting, wherever possible, a practical collaboration with other Churches, Orthodox ecumenism will always give the first place to problems of faith, since it is faith alone which ultimately brings about *true* unity. Catholic ecumenism, on the contrary, especially in its relations with Orthodoxy, will tend (consciously or unconsciously) to minimize doctrinal problems with the one exception of Roman primacy—the necessary sign of belonging to the Church. This primacy, however, is frequently held to be compatible with the most far-reaching doctrinal, liturgical and practical liberalism. The astonishing flexibility of so many Roman Catholic theologians and ecumenists is explained often by their knowledge that the ultimate responsibility for truth does not belong to them and that obedience to Rome gives them the final security to do and say *anything* which the magisterium has not formally prohibited.

The modern ecumenism of the Roman Church, as defined in the appropriate Constitution of Vatican II, rests on a major affirmation found in the first Chapter: valid Christian elements manifested outside the visible unity of the Catholic Church—the written Word, the Sacraments, faith, charity, hope, the fruits of the Holy Spirit—belong in fact and "by right" to the one Church of Christ. A flat *no* is hereby tendered to the negativists who—although disavowed for some time on the doctrinal level—have nevertheless continued to act on the practical level as if there were no grace or salvation outside the Roman Church. At the same time, however, the Church also takes the offensive: she affirms her "right" to all forms of authentic Christianity, a "right" which, of course, concerned parties do not recognize, but which has objective value nonetheless. Thus, since any "valid" Sacrament is "by right" a Sacrament of the Church and since this validity is a fact more important than its recognition or non-recognition by the one who receives it, so then ecclesiastical authority can admit, in certain cases, the practice of *communio in sacris* with separated Christians. Used with "discernment," this sacramental communion can even be regarded as a "means" of attaining unity (Chapter II).

Although some Catholic ecumenists were defending this concept of "inter-communion" before the Council, it is evident that the decisions of Vatican II on this point are quite revolutionary. For forty years Orthodox participants of the Ecumenical Movement have tried to persuade the Protestants to admit the view which sees the Eucharist as the sign *per excellence* of *realized* unity, thus excluding any form of intercommunion between separated communities. For the Orthodox, sacramental communion represents, in fact, a commitment to the whole Christ who is "the Way, the Truth, and the Life." This wholeness is objectively present in the one Church, and so it is there and there only that the commitment can be made. Inversely, the Church cannot admit to the Sacraments those who consciously refuse the fullness of Christian truth.[6] All theories of "intercommunion" presuppose, therefore, either some form of relativism or a theological disjunction between the sacramental presence of Christ and His revelation as unique Truth.

Modern Roman Catholic ecumenism finds itself, apparently, in just this latter position. The juridical notion of the Church, which sees the Church as a universal structure controlling and guaranteeing doctrine, separates the sacramental Christ from the Truth. So, then, the Constitution *De ecumenismo,* although it is somewhat evasive with regard to Protestants—it does, however, mention the possibility of a *communio in sacris* within certain disciplinary limits — actually ends up by encouraging "intercommunion" in the case of the Orthodox in view of the sacramental validity of the episcopate which it has preserved (Chapter III). And yet, *De ecclesia* (III,22) specifies that bishops who are not in communion with the See of Rome have no doctrinal authority whatever. The thought of the Council seems perfectly clear on this point: doctrinal authority and sacramental reality are distinct entities, and there is, therefore, no obstacle (other than disciplinary considerations) to intercommunion in cases where the validity of the Sacraments is recognized within the life of the separated community. This is also the dominant point of view in the Protestant world, and there could be no better illustration of A. S. Khomiakov's paradoxical assertion: "Romanism was protestant at its very origin."[7]

Orthodox opposition to all forms of intercommunion [8] does not, of course, mean a denial of Christ's presence in non-Orthodox communities. It does imply a radical refusal to admit any kind of division *in Christ.* If such a division is a fact in the separated Churches, insofar as they break down in one way or another the fullness of catholic truth, Orthodoxy cannot enter into any form of sacramental communion with them, for it does not admit that the Body of Christ in which, through Baptism, an Orthodox Christian finds full communion with God can be divided. Every partial presence of redemptive grace must find its accomplishment, its fullness in the bosom of the one Church. This is what happens when communities or individuals who have received Baptism and other Sacraments outside Orthodoxy are admitted into the Church without the repetition of these Sacraments.

Such an attitude is in no way opposed to ecumenism; on the contrary, it expresses an unswerving fidelity to the cause of true unity which cannot be achieved through compromise on the basis of some "minimum," but implies a union "in Christ" in the fullness both of revelation and the sacramental presence—which are *inseparable*. The catholicity of the Church implies that every division between "life" and "truth" is also a division of Christ: Christian unity is, therefore, essentially a living unity in and with Christ, and it is precisely this fact that Orthodoxy expresses when it refuses to separate truth from the Sacraments.

This disjunction is the inherent danger of all "reductions" of catholic ecclesiology within this or that particular aspect of the Church's life. True catholicity lies, in fact, in an organic wholeness, wherein each aspect of the Church represents not a part but a form or aspect of the totality. Even a so-called "Eucharistic ecclesiology" can succumb to the same temptation: that of identifying the Church with the sacramental presence to the point of forgetting what this presence implies. Thus we can see a truly paradoxical coincidence, in favor of intercommunion, between a Eucharistic "extremism," such as that of Father Afanassiev[9] (who otherwise represents one of the most interesting modern attempts to restore the primitive notion of the Church), and the ecumenism of Vatican II, based as it is on the principle, diametrically opposed to Afanassiev's, of a universal Church exercising its "right" to all that is authentically Christian wherever it may be found. In each case, but for the opposite reasons, sacramental communion is separated from communion in the Truth.

The debate on intercommunion is a good illustration of the basic ecclesiological problem raised between Rome and Orthodoxy, and it leads us inevitably to the definitions of primacy, episcopacy and collegiality which are found in Chapter III of the Constitution *De ecclesia*.

Every Orthodox Christian must, to begin with, welcome the fact that the Constitution is a reply under several headings to the preoccupation with the nature of the episcopate which has been growing in the Roman Church since 1870. It formally disavows the tendency which would consider the bishop as a local delegate of the pope and proclaims the episcopate as a permanent institution of the Church, the highest sacerdotal order (III, 26), and as exercising "also," collectively, the infallible magisterium of the Church (III, 25). This infallibility resides also, in a certain sense, in the *corpus fidelium,* whose universal consensus—a "supernatural discernment sustained by the Spirit of Truth"—cannot err in questions of faith and morals (II,12). Reading these texts one can only rediscover the whole breadth and genuine depth of our common share in the unique tradition of the primitive Church, the Church of the Councils and the Fathers.

However, the Constitution also contains a number of rather clearly expressed conclusions which put these views on collegiality, primacy and infallibility—at first glance apparently shared with us—in a quite different light. The words themselves acquire a different meaning.

One of the foundations of primitive Christian ecclesiology—still essential to Orthodoxy—is the notion that the local Church, as a sacramental community, is the Body of Christ in all its fullness. It was in the light of this view that St. Cyprian asserted that every bishop sits on "the seat of Peter," and held, therefore, that the succession from Peter was an attribute of every local Church. It is precisely on these grounds that the Church has always recognized the bishop as the *summit* of the Church's hierarchy (and the Council's recognition of this point provides us with a common theological ground for the dialogue to come). We know, of course, that Cyprian was also the great doctor of episcopal collegiality, but he connected this notion with the functional *identity* of the bishops;[19] a bishop cannot legitimately preside over his Church if his equals have not recognized him in the function he is exercising.

Is *this* the notion of episcopacy which is found in the Constitution *De ecclesia?*

In its third chapter, the Constitution provides a good description of the episcopal function as a function of "eucharistic ecclesiology" and formally admits that a Christian community gathered around the bishop and the Eucharistic table is "the one, holy, catholic and apostolic Church" by virtue of the presence of Christ in its midst (III, 26) ; but other passages clearly reject the seemingly necessary consequences stemming from these premises. We read that the local Churches are built "on the model of the universal Church," as "parts" of the universal Church, and the mystical Body is therefore also "a body of Churches" (III, 23). Without entering here into the question whether such a use of the Pauline notion of the Body is legitimate, it is enough to note that, if the local sacramental communities are only "parts," they are not going to see themselves as "the catholic Church" in its local manifestation.

These contradictions, whether real or apparent, in the Council's text, clearly show that its authors have seriously considered the theology of the local Church as a "catholic" reality. They have even tried, apparently, to give it the greatest credit possible—and this will undoubtedly provide another point of departure for the future dialogue with Orthodoxy. But it is symptomatic that this theology of the local Church is in no way used to define the very *nature* of the episcopate, for example in terms of the thought of St. Ignatius of Antioch, but is merely considered as a framework for the exercise of episcopal *functions,* while the *origin* of the episcopate is defined exclusively by the doctrine of apostolic succession. And yet, as we have tried to show repeatedly, the doctrine of apostolic succession, traced to its Christian origins, is an integral part of a communal and sacramental ecclesiology. It existed as an inherent function of each local "catholic" Church, and did not by any means imply a simple identification of episcopacy with apostolicity. The episcopal office—in Ignatius, Irenaeus, Cyprian and the whole subsequent liturgical and canonical tradition in the West, as in the East— is, first of all, a function of the local Church. It is his sacramental, magisterial and pastoral function in a particular community which qualifies the bishop to participate in the college of the universal episcopate. Participation in the college is of course a necessary element in the function of the bishop and a sign of the authenticity of his episcopacy—the collegial character of episcopal ordination bears clear witness to this—, but it is for his local Church and within its very bosom, confirmed by the communion and witness of all the other Churches, that the episcopate is given to him. He is not an apostle who, by some chance, in the course of his wandering evangelical ministry or by virtue of a commission conferred upon him by some "ecclesiastical superiors" temporarily governs a diocese. He is an essential element of the very Body of the local Church, of its "catholicity" and its "apostolicity," and it is by virtue of these functions that the apostolic succession is bestowed on him by his brothers in the episcopate.

The problem of the "universal" and the "sacramental" in ecclesiology is certainly crucial and one which probably cannot be resolved on an exclusively logical or juridical level. It is true that one form of "Eucharistic ecclesiology," overly schematized and simplified, tends to forget the "universal" dimension of the Church along with all that this imples, notably the necessary Christian witness, both in the world and as a function of the world as it exists. On the other hand, Vatican II, despite certain appearances to the contrary, has in no way modified the position which has dominated western Christianity since the fall of the Roman Empire, and it is building its ecclesiology as a function of the universal mission of the Church, not as a function of the Church's sacramental nature.

The constant references to the rights of the Church of Rome, the repeated affirmation that only within the Roman obedience—in constant obedience to its ordinary *magisterium* and not just to its decisions *ex cathedra* (III, 25) —is the ecclesiological character of a particular Church manifested, clearly indicate what "makes the Church to be the Church" in the mind of the Council: i.e., unity with the See of Rome. It is evident also that the collegiality of the bishops is rigorously subordinated to this essential criterion, which in fact gives the Roman Church today its effectiveness and prestige in the eyes if not of the best, then, at least, of the majority of its members.

This subordination is expressed not only in the passages which sum up the definitions of infallibility, but especially in those which speak of the ordinary power of the bishops. Thus the bishop can exercise within his diocese the powers given to him by custom, but only if these powers have not been revoked by Rome (III, 24). It is evident, then, that not only are national, patriarchal, etc., privileges (such as those which the "united" eastern Churches are making so much of today, and for which Patriarch Maximos IV Sayegh was carrying on such a stubborn fight) —not only are these at the theoretical and practical mercy of the See of Rome, but the exercise of the episcopate itself in all its forms depends on Rome's good will. And although the definition of Vatican I of the "episcopal" and "immediate" jurisdiction of the pope over all the pastors and the faithful of the universal Church, considered both collectively and individually, is not actually repeated in so many words, still it is no less clearly affirmed in the following words: "The college of the body of bishops has no authority unless it is understood together with the Roman Pontiff... the pope's power of primacy over all, both pastors and faithful, remains whole and intact" (III, 22).

Thus, as we have pointed out above, the Council does not consider the episcopal office itself as a delegation of papal powers, and yet the *exercise* of the episcopate is still placed in total dependence on the Roman Pontiff, and this by divine right.

What, then, is left of the concept of collegiality? Its essential character resides primarily, it would seem, in the fact that it enters into the framework of the universal canonical structure of which the pope is the head. The bishops are members of the college by being individually joined to it (and in practice by virtue of a choice exercised by Rome), and not as heads of their particular Churches. They represent the college in their dioceses, but not their communities in the midst of the whole body of Churches. As strict a parallel as possible is drawn between the choice of the apostles by the Lord and the mechanics of collegiality. But, as we have seen, the bishops are not apostles. The sacramental bond of bishop-and-community is what makes the difference. A sound concept of episcopacy presupposes a double representation: the bishop is, *at the same time,* the man of his particular Church within the universal college and, by virtue of the apostolic succession in his diocese and of his participation in the college, the representative of God in his Church. If one of the elements of this balance is excluded, there is a fall either into congregationalism or into a concept of the Church which applies the image of the local community to the universal Church, that is, a single "universal" bishop surrounded by a college of presbyter-bishops. Such, in fact, was the picture evolved by Vatican I, and, alas, it remains basically the same after Vatican II.

It is certainly clear—and Orthodoxy should recognize this—that the mere existence of a universal college implies a certain structure, indeed a *primus,* whose priority is not necessarily just a primacy of honor. The college can, and even should, have a head, nor can the head be independent of the college, since the latter must constantly be recognized in its chief representative. The 34th "apostolic canon" has this to say, for example, on the subject of local primacies: "The bishops of every nation must acknowledge him who is first among them and account him as their head, and do nothing of consequence without his consent. . . But neither let him (who is the first) do anything without the consent of all; for so there will be unanimity, and God will be glorified through the Lord in the Holy Spirit."[11] This same principle must necessarily be applied to the idea of universal primacy (whether of Rome or Constantinople). The absence of any *interdependence* between the pope and the bishops in the decisions of Vatican II actually deprives the texts on collegiality of much real value.

It was probably out of the question to think that the Council would proclaim such an interdependence. Each bishop, according to the Council, is in fact the pastor of a "part" of the Church, while the bishop of Rome is the head of the "whole" (III, 18). This "whole" can, of course, be governed either in an autocratic or a democratic manner, but, being a "whole," it must control its parts. The ancient Church saw in each bishop the head of the "whole" manifested locally, and this "whole" was not a geographical concept—the universal Church of 150 or 1966—but the Body of Christ which includes infinitely more members than the empirical and visible Church can count today, since it includes the Mother of God, the angels, and the whole communion of saints. This Body is not a geographical universality, with an "infallible" disciplinary center (that is, a human structure), but the assembly of the faithful inspired by the Spirit of Truth and whose actual number is theologically of secondary importance. "Wherever Christ Jesus is, there is the Catholic Church," wrote Ignatius of Antioch *(Smyr.* 8:2); and Irenaeus is just as clear: "Where the Church is, there is the Spirit of God; and where the Spirit of God is, there is the Church, and every kind of grace; but the Spirit is truth."[12]

Thus, ontologically, there are no superiors and inferiors within the college of bishops, each one presides locally over the whole Body. The canonical and disciplinary structures, however, both local and universal, are all defined by the college itself and by the needs for witness, for common action, or in general by the needs of the life of the Church in the world. In Byzantium it was even admitted that they could be defined by the Emperor.

We know that historically the Roman centralization developed in the "void" created in the West by the disappearance of the Christian Roman Empire, and since then it has always been determined by the need—which Orthodoxy must learn to respect—for an effective witness in history. Western ecclesiology has been and remains "cosmocentric." Its essential preoccupation is "this world," into which the Lord has sent His apostles, a world which is called to become, ultimately, the Kingdom of God. It is as a function of the needs and also, alas, of the *categories* of this world that it is often defined. Hence its constant juridical emphasis, its search for a criterion, for doctrinal clarity and formal discipline. Hence also the partial checkmate of the great movement unleashed by John XXIII. Now while the preoccupation to save the world is a legitimate and necessary preoccupation—the Church exists *for* the world—it is still true that it is by revealing *new* realities to the world, *new* spiritual categories, which the world does not and cannot possess on its own, rather than by accepting the world's laws and logic, that this salvation will be realized.

We do not yet know how collegiality will actually function, since the Council agreed that the pope should put these decisions into practice at his own discretion. The manner in which he dealt with the Assembly in the final two days of the third session gives us good cause to assume that he intends to fully exercise the powers that the Council has not actually put in question. Perhaps some day the idea of the "collective infallibility" of the episcopate, in spite of the tremendous precautions which have been taken to safeguard the authority of the Sovereign Pontiff, will ring about some unexpected development, and create a real counter-balance to papal supremacy. Theological reflection, the gradual rediscovery of the ancient and common tradition of the Church, and in the end simply historical circumstances, can perhaps give some practical meaning to what today seems a trifle "out of context." Ecumenical events of recent years have introduced so much (perhaps too much) that is spectacular and unexpected that the ultimate achievement which Providence may assign to our efforts toward unity may well go beyond any current calculations.

POPE AND PATRIARCH

The lifting of the excommunications of 1054, proclaimed simultaneously in Rome and Istanbul was probably the most spectacular event concluding the last session of Vatican II. Press headlines caused some people even to think that the schism was over. The agreed-upon statement issued by Athenagoras I and Paul VI was very carefully drafted, however, and described the event simply as a "gesture of good will." It even included an implicit retreat from the position on "intercommunion" previously and unilaterally taken by the Council, and it specified that *communio in sacris* is to be preceded by a serious dialogue and a full agreement on issues of faith. There is no doubt that such is the only procedure acceptable to the Orthodox.

In order to understand its value properly, it must first be recalled that, formally, the schism cannot be dated as of 1054; in fact, it cannot strictly be dated at all. It is now universally agreed by Church historians that the incident which occurred in 1054 between Patriarch Michael Cerullarios and Cardinal Humbert, legate of Pope Leo IX, was not the actual beginning of schism so much as an unsuccessful attempt at reconciliation.[13]

Communion between Constantinople and Rome had been broken since the first years of the eleventh century, mainly for political reasons, possibly also in connection with Rome's acceptance in 1014 of the *Filioque* clause in the Creed. At any rate, the contemporaries considered the situation as a conflict between two Patriarchates, not two "Churches." Other Patriarchs, those of Alexandria, of Antioch, and of Jerusalem, seem to have remained in communion with both sides, at least for some time after 1054.

What actually happened in 1054? The legates, whose mission was reconciliation, got involved in a dispute on liturgy and discipline, for which the Byzantine Patriarch was also largely responsible. Should one fast on Saturdays? Should one use leavened or unleavened bread for Communion? Such were the issues debated by the two sides, both unable either to understand the motives of the adversary or to lift the debate to a constructive level. In the background, of course, the sides were already separated by the fundamental ecclesiological issue: Is Rome the final criterion of Christian truth? The Byzantines were not ready to recognize it as such, and this explains why they were always ready to challenge the Westerners, even on secondary and trivial matters.

The excommunication which the legates finally deposited on the altar of St. Sophia was directed at "Michael and his followers,"[14] and this can obviously be understood as covering the whole Orthodox Church. In retaliation the Patriarch excommunicated only "the impious document and its authors,"[15] specifically avoiding inclusion in his action of the Bishop of Rome or the western Church as a whole.

These were the excommunications lifted in 1965. On the Orthodox side, only the Patriarch of Constantinople was involved, and not the whole Eastern Church: Patriarch Athenagoras was, therefore, at least in principle, entitled to act by himself and to cancel the action of his predecessor. Not being, in any sense, an Orthodox pope, he could not speak on behalf of the whole of Orthodoxy. Michael Cerullarios, in 1054, had an immensely greater *de facto* power over the Orthodox world of that time than does Athenagoras I today, but even he was not followed blindly by all. And, in any case, only Humbert and his companions were the objects of the Byzantine anathema, and it is only this particular excommunication which was lifted in 1965.

The canonical significance of the action taken by Paul VI could be interpreted as having wider significance if one isolates the events of 1054 from subsequent history. However, such an isolation is obviously impossible. From the Roman Catholic point of view, the Orthodox remain under excommunication through numerous actions taken by Rome since 1054: the Orthodox Church does not recognize, for example, the decision of Lyons (1274), of Florence (1440), of Trent (1542–1563), of Vatican I (1870), and all these assemblies have imitated the early Church Councils in that they conclude each of their definitions by a definite *anathema sit* against those who reject them. These anathemas, from the Roman point of view, still apply to the Orthodox, and inversely, the Orthodox continue to reject the Roman "innovations." All of which shows quite clearly that the decision of 1965 does not change anything in the canonical and sacramental relations between Orthodoxy and Rome.

Actually, it is quite clear that the problem is not a canonical one which can be solved through some formal action by the "appropriate Church authorities": issues of faith are not solved in that way. Unity can be achieved only in a common vision of the whole Truth, and it is quite evident that this has not yet been achieved. A thorough and honest dialogue, in an atmosphere of mutual trust, must first take place. The "gesture of good will" by Athenagoras and Paul VI may contribute to that end, especially if it is interpreted in its true light: a moral commitment, taken by both sides, to avoid mutual slander and misunderstandings due to ignorance and to start a dialogue on the real issues, with due respect to the other side's convictions. The events of 1054 constitute a model—almost a caricature—of how the problem of union should not be handled. It is a good thing that—also symbolically—it has been "given to oblivion."

How immensely more significant, for example, would be the restoration in the list of the Ecumenical Councils recognized by Rome of the Council of Constantinople of 879-880, the only really *successful* attempt at union between east and west. For one of the most exciting results of contemporary historical research (especially the studies by F. Dvornik) has been the discovery that this council, sponsored and approved by Patriarch Photius and Pope John VIII, had remained in the western lists of Ecumenical Councils until the eleventh century when the Latin canonists arbitrarily replaced it with the Council of 869–870.[16] A decision of this sort would certainly change *fundamentally* the relations between Orthodoxy and Rome.

CONCLUSIONS

As it faces the Christian West today, the Orthodox Church certainly has its task cut out for it—the task of making it plain that its "theocentric" ecclesiology is indeed that which the Lord willed to reveal to his faithful. Certain paradoxes in the concrete life of Orthodoxy seem unfortunately to justify the doubts which the West often has concerning the seriousness of our convictions. The tragic situation in which political events have engulfed a large part of the Orthodox world with persecutions (which, since 1959, continue to reduce in numbers and means the membership of the Church in Russia) also gives us little hope or consolation. All this is nothing less than a test of that "theocentrism" on which we have relied so poorly, but which we cherish even more when it is being questioned.

In our relations with our Roman Catholic brothers, we must, above all, try to rid ourselves mutually of a number of misunderstandings which too often cloud sound theological reflection and obstruct true dialogue.

Orthodox Christians must, on their part, rid themselves of the idea that Roman ecclesiology can be reduced to an insatiable thirst for power and that, consequently, all we need do is restrict papal jurisdiction to the West and repress "uniatism" in the East in order that the two Churches might live in peace. To nourish such ideas is to do a real injury to our Roman Catholic brothers. For them, the Papacy is not a form of imperialism—even though the Middle Ages often made it appear as such—but an article of faith, a divine gift bestowed for the well-being of the Church, and which, out of an authentic love for us and a sincere zeal for the Lord, they want us to share. The unionist efforts of Vatican II clearly encouraged a search for a solution which would permit us to accept this gift without mourning. It is essential for our future dialogue that we understand this and take the Roman Catholic position seriously.

But Rome also must remove certain false problems and misunderstandings from its ecumenism. One of these is the conviction, real or apparent, in many Catholic circles that the schism can be overcome by a simple restoration, within the limits of Roman unity, of the liturgical traditions and ways of the Christian East. The particular emphasis with which the Constitution *De ecumenismo* speaks of the "venerable eastern liturgies," the very real efforts made to de-Latinize certain hybrid rites in use in the uniat Churches, the remarkably scholarly publications which are restoring and interpreting the true meaning of the eastern liturgy—all these will come to nothing if they do not bring about a true theological confrontation which will go well beyond the historical East/West problem and will put Rome herself in question as to the criterion of faith. Whatever in Orthodox theology is truly authentic, whatever is at the depths of the instinct of popular piety in the Orthodox world is not simply liturgical conservatism or a desire to preserve an Orthodox form of Christianity threatened by the Latin West, but a conception of the Church that is valid for both West and East, a "catholic" faith which not only continues the eastern tradition, but responds also to the legitimate aspirations of the Reformers and represents, therefore, the resolution of the drama which has divided the West since the sixteenth century. As J-J. von Allmen writes: "What the Reformed Churches expect of the Orthodox Churches is, therefore, that they should try to convince Rome, which is so anxious today not to offend them, that in their eyes it does not comprise the whole of western Christianity, that it must therefore. in a way that is not only diplomatic but also theologically new, begin to re-examine the Reformation of the sixteenth century."[17]

Seen in this perspective, the patronizing words about "venerable liturgies" and the quarrels of protocol revolving on the question whether the uniat Patriarchs should or should not take precedence over the Roman cardinals really do seem to lack seriousness, while the justified indignation which seized certain Fathers of the Council (Latin Fathers) in the face of some realities of the Roman curia represents a real hope, even though the concerned parties refuse at present to recognize the true ecclesiological dimensions of the drama in which they are taking part.

To bring about an understanding of these dimensions: here is the truly ecumenical task of Orthodox theology today. This is not a merely intellectual task, nor even one that is solely ecumenical. It requires also a realization, within the Orthodox Church herself, of conditions which would manifest in practice the reality to which we claim to bear witness.

NOTES

[1] P.L., 77, col. 739 A.

[2] *Ibid.*, 746 C.

[3] On this subject see *The Primacy of Peter in the Orthodox*

Church, London, 1963, a collection of recent articles by a group of Orthodox theologians; see also *St. Vladimir's Quarterly,* Vol. 4, 1960, No. 2–3, a volume dedicated to *Primacy and Primacies.*

[4] *Cf.*, on this subject, R. Aubert, *"L'ecclésiologie du concile du Vatican,"* in *Le Concile et les Conciles* (Cerf), 1960, p. 281.

[5] *Ibid.*, pp. 283–284.

[6] A study of the numerous cases of intercommunion between Roman Catholics and Orthodox during the sixteenth and seventeenth centuries is to be found in Timothy Ware, *Eustratios Argenti, A Study of the Greek Church under Turkish Rule,* Oxford, 1964. The cases were generally due to political considerations, or misunderstanding, or simple ignorance. They ultimately led to the very extremes of mutual bitterness and animosity.

[7] *L'Eglise latine et le protestantisme au point du vue de L'Eglise d'Orient. Recueil d'articles sur des questions réligieuses écrits à différentes époques et à différentes occasions,* Lausanne et Vevey, 1872, p. 36.

[8] "The Eucharistic Mystery is the end of unity, not a means to that end and . . . therefore the decisions regarding Holy Communion reached by Christian bodies outside the Orthodox Church have no significance or validity for the Orthodox Church or her members. Holy Communion will not be sought by Orthodox Christians outside of the Church, nor will it be offered to those who do not yet confess the Orthodox Church as their Mothers." Statement on "The Discipline of Holy Communion."

[9] *Una sancta,* in *Irénikon,* XXXVI, 1963, 4, pp. 436–475.

[10] This concept of the episcopate is today almost universally recognized in Cyprian; *cf.*, for example, M. Bévenot's commentary on Cyprian's *De Unitate* in *Ancient Christian Writers,* 25, The Newman Press, Westminster, Md., 1957.

[11] The Nicene and Post-Nicene Fathers, Grand Rapids, Michigan, 1956, Vol. XIV, p. 596. The so-called "apostolic canons" receive their authority from their endorsement by the Council *in Trullo* (692), or "Quinisext." In this canon, the word "nation" is to be understood in a territorial and not in an ethnic sense.

[12] *Adv. Haer.* III, 24, 1; *The Nicene and Post-Nicene Fathers,* I, New York, 1925, p. 458.

[13] On the events of 1054, see a symposium published in commemoration of the 900th anniversary of those events and offered to a well-known Roman Catholic unionist, Dom Lambert Beauduin:

L'Eglise et les églises, 2 vols., Ed. de Chévetogne, 1955; see also Stephen Runciman, *The Eastern Schism,* Oxford, 1955.

[14] P.L., CXLIII, 1002.

[15] P.G., CXX, 748 B.

[16] F. Dvornik, *The Photian Schism. History and Legend,* Cambridge, 1948.

[17] "A Protestant Appeal to the Orthodox," in *St. Vladimir's Seminary Quarterly,* Vol. 9, 1965, n° 1, p. 13.

INDEX